DOUG CLARK

THE COMING

OIL

WAR

PREDICTIONS OF THINGS TO COME

Please return to :
Arne Kasel
Herbster, Wis

HARVEST HOUSE PUBLISHERS
Irvine, California 92714

THE COMING OIL WAR

Copyright © 1980 by Harvest House Publishers
Irvine, California 92714

Library of Congress Catalog Card Number 79-56820
ISBN 0-89081-226-8

The views presented by the author of the book do not necessarily represent the views of the Publisher.

Printed in the United States of America.

THIS BOOK IS DEDICATED

to the sincere American people,
who love this country
and its free-enterprise system.

It is dedicated to those people
who believe wholeheartedly
in the freedoms we cherish and cling to,
more than any other nation on earth.

Doug Clark

ABOUT THE AUTHOR

TV commentator Doug Clark has been specializing in the study of economics, political science, and future events for over 20 years. He has done graduate work at Holmes Theological Seminary and the University of Toronto, and has traveled extensively around the world.

Doug and his wife, Charlene, are currently involved in seminars on future survival and the alarming developments in the money markets. His books and newsletters combine a penetrating analysis of biblical predictions with both financial and political forecasting, and are proving invaluable to thousands of people in our age of uncertainty.

Doug Clark is a prolific author, and his new best-seller, HOW TO SURVIVE THE MONEY CRASH, is must reading along with THE COMING OIL WAR.

CONTENTS

Chapter 1
The War Scenario

It was 2:00 P.M. in New York, 11:00 A.M. in Los Angeles, and 8:00 A.M. in Hawaii when all hell broke loose in Jerusalem.

Small missiles were dropping in carefully placed destinations every four minutes.

Pandemonium broke loose in Tel Aviv, Haifa, and West Jerusalem. Mayor Teddy Kollek picked up the red phone and dialed a prearranged number that range in 17 offices of the members of the Knesset, including the Prime Minister of Israel and his cabinet and party members.

"We're being pulverized by enemy missiles! This is the red alert! Mobilize and help us immediately."

To get a call on that line meant only one thing to each of them: this was an emergency of national proportions, and that could only mean an act of Jehovah or the dreaded PLO.

It was the PLO.

The Predictions

More than one minister in the Knesset had predicted along with the Prime Minister that war would come soon. Military alert had been sounded months before, and every able-bodied man and woman had been conscripted, trained, and equipped. They took their weapons and wore their uniforms to work every day while carrying on their civilian positions and responsibilities (after a crash training course involving tough training and tight discipline). Each Israeli knew that it was the life-and-death-of-Israel battle coming up.

The military attack came through Lebanon, Syria, and Jordan, with troops coming from Iran, Iraq, and Saudi Arabia. Further away, Moslem troops and military equipment were being shipped in from Moamar Gaddafi, Pakistan, Kuwait, and the United Arab ministates of the Persian Gulf.

Reports had it that North and South Yemen were sending contingencies of men, along with Somalia and Ethiopia.

The big news was that Soviet weaponry was everywhere, with large battalions of Soviet-armed-troops, should the Arabs fail in their all-out attempt to conquer Israel, take the West Bank, and Jerusalem, and drive the Israelis to the sea.

Failing this, the Soviets were committed to more than just supervision of the coordination of Arab battalions; they were committed to fight to the finish regardless of the American-European position.

Prior to this dreadful hour, negotiations had gone on for weeks between the warring parties over the areas of the West Bank and Jerusalem.

Israel was adamant. She had gone far enough in giving land back. Sadat and Begin had accomplished the opening of borders between these great warring countries of the past. Peace had come between them: Israel had given much land back.

Pandemonium in the U.S.

The U.S. had struggled in these negotiations to virtually force Israel to acquiesce to the Arab demands, for the Arabs had started to cut back oil shipments to the U.S.

The U.S. was hurting badly. They were suffering their own economic Armageddon in these days of lessening oil supplies from the chief suppliers in the Middle East.

Canada was helping the United States through the direct negotiations of their new Prime Minister, who was deeply committed to helping his neighbor to the south. After all, as goes the United States, so goes Canada.

Mexico had stepped up supplies of oil, but this was not sufficient to ward off the greatest depression in the history of the U.S. No President could stop it, nor could congress. Their hands were tied by not having developed nuclear power soon enough to make the U.S. self-sufficient in energy. But that was hindsight now.

The emergency was on. Countless businesses were shut down, hundreds of others had gone out of business, and still others had declared bankruptcy.

Economic pandemonium had broken out in the most powerful nation in the world.

American politicians had tried to force the Israelies into giving in, having been delivered the ultimatum from Saudi Arabia and OPEC to force them to capitulate or else lose shipments of oil to the U.S. until they did.

Nothing worked.

Now, with economic confusion in the country, and with no power demonstrated at the peace conferences between

Israel and the Arabs, the U.S. was suffering the worst it ever had.

Crime was on the rampage as people begged, borrowed, and stole to eat and live.

The auto industry was shut down. Steel mills ground to a halt. Entertainment centers folded. Lake Tahoe and Reno rolled up the carpet and went to bed. Las Vegas was holding on by a thread. No one was thinking pleasure; it was all just existence—"How will we survive this?"

Suicides were up to an all-time high. People in all walks of life were feeling the terrible squeeze.

The government was mobilizing for war; energy needs were going in that direction.

Hawaii was on full alert for Soviet submarines in the region, and NORAD was constantly watching for a full-scale surprise Soviet attack. All U.S. military watchdogs were on full alert.

The Call to War

That did it.

Millions paraded in the street, demanding that the government declare war on the Arabs immediately.

Just a few years earlier, the Americans had extricated themselves from a volatile political situation called Vietnam. The people and the politicians said unanimously, "Never another war on foreign soil."

But this was different. Ties were close in the Judeo-Christian circles of American heritage. Even closer was the need to eat, work, and pursue happiness with Arab oil!

Millions were demonstrating to fight the Arabs, and the country was ready in spirit and optimism. After weeks of the dragging depression getting worse and worse, the people were united like one gigantic family on one monumental issue—*fight to get oil now!*

The President responded with congress. We declared war! It was the GREAT OIL WAR.

Chapter 2
The Grim Facts

Does the preceding scenario sound impossible to you? It is not impossible at all. Many senators will tell you it is their secret dread.

Higher up the military line are the generals, like General G.J. Keegan, Jr., a retired Air Force Major General who said he resigned from the service because of government cover-up of the imminency of a Soviet attack on America. He said he did everything within the service to alert everyone to the danger, but finally had to resign to be heard. Now he is exhausting every potential in alerting Americans to the fact that the Soviets are ready for war with the world, due to our helping them mobilize.

"After 60 years of aggression by the Soviets, only 17 percent of the remaining world population lives in what could be termed a free society, and the rate of decline of that percentage is 6 percent!" The General, a former assistant Chief of Staff for Air Force Intelligence, concludes that the Soviets are going through the most extensive war preparations in history.

Many other renowned Americans, Canadians, English and French sources say the same thing, but we don't seem to be listening to them. The news media treat those warnings as trivia from fanatics.

The following pages document and present the story of the oil cartels and their twin powers on earth and in the American system. You will learn WHY WE WILL FIGHT THIS WAR SOON. You will be able to see WHO GAVE THE SOVIETS THEIR POWER TO FIGHT US TODAY.

You will also be able to ascertain WHAT HAS PLAC-
ED US IN THIS PRECARIOUS ENERGY POSITION
OF RELIANCE ON A FOREIGN POWER.

Armed with the Facts

I want to remind you of the following facts.

1. There are two oil cartels—not just one.
2. The domestic cartel is interlocked with the eight
   biggest banks in positions of interlocking directorships.
3. We have ridiculously *not developed our own
   energy sources.*
4. It was predicted by Lenin and Ezekial that we
   would fight Russia. We will.
5. As result we will have an economic Armageddon
   here first.
6. There will be a massive war between the superpowers, using conventional and nuclear weapons
   to the ultimate.
7. I am thoroughly convinced that we will win this
   oil war with the Arabs and the Soviets, but we
   will come out bleeding badly.
8. *You can survive this oil war and come out on
   top.*

Once you are armed with the following facts on who
controls oil here and abroad, you will be better able to
understand all the complex maze of reasons for this
unavoidable oil war.

For instance, if it were not for the myriad of government
regulations on the "seven sisters" (oil companies) and the
other companies in the energy businesses, we would have
plenty of energy today in America and would never need to
go to war to secure it.

In addition, were it not for the unbelievable (mostly hidden) financial and scientific aid given to the technological-
ly impoverished Soviets by our own capitalistic system, we

would not have to fight this war. Communism would be dead by now, without capitalists keeping it alive!

America needs energy more than any other nation on earth because of our industrial giants, our great way of life, and our constant aggressive outreach toward new horizons and science. That's the kind of people we are. We are not prepared to go back to the caves. We will fight rather than do that.

Here are the cold, hard, unknown facts.

The Shocking Facts

1. The costs per barrel of oil are soaring monthly as OPEC (Organization of Petroleum Exporting Countries) jacks up the costs for nations everywhere.

2. They are hiking the price of oil because the dollar is dying in its intrinsic purchasing power weekly on the open markets of the foreign exchange.

3. The dollar is dying because the Federal Reserve System in collaboration with the federal government is printing too many dollars compared to the declining GNP (Gross National Product—accumulated values of services and goods produced in this country).

4. Inflation of the dollar means less purchasing power for the dollar, so that the Arabs are getting exactly the same purchasing power per dollar in 1979 that they had in 1975. This is why the price hikes are coming.

5. The average American home uses 1806 gallons (43 barrels) of oil per year, according to Phillips Petroleum Company.

About 45 percent of this is used to produce electricity, 35 percent for space heating, 12 percent for cooling, and 8 percent for heating water.

6. Currently the U.S. oil bill is close to 55 billion dollars, compared to last year's bill of 42 billion dollars. Unless there is a drastic change in inflation of the dollar and the usage of oil in North America, we are headed for a 100-billion-dollar yearly budget for energy in U.S.

7. The way salaries are going up, and the way the unemployment statistics are rising (due to layoffs and cutbacks in industry), the American public cannot afford to pay this bill for oil without great changes in our society and standard of living. The age of wealth and affluence is over.

8. Skyrocketing food prices reflect the government's inflationary policies with respect to printing the dollar.

9. Skyrocketing real estate prices in some areas also reflect the Federal Reserve System's policy of printing too much money.

10. As Americans work from January to June 10 each year, this money is paid directly into local, state, and federal taxes.

11. There are two cartels controlling oil in the world. One is the cartel known as OPEC that you have been aware of. The other is the organization known as the "seven sisters." These are: EXXON, MOBIL, STANDARD OIL OF INDIANA, SOCAL (STANDARD OIL OF CALIFORNIA), SHELL, TEXACO, AND ARCO.

12. The former cartel controls what comes out of the ground and how much is deliverable to the nations. The latter cartel controls what is distributed to the U.S. and how much is refined into gas, heating oil, etc., and they control the complete operation of oil from—

    A) the original possession of the reserves of oil in this country, by virtue of bringing it in or producing it domestically;

    B) the production of crude oil in this nation;

    C) the refining of the crude oil into the products desired—gasoline, oil, fertilizers, and 300 other products for American usage;

    D) the final sales of the products, through gasoline dealers retail sales of other products through their subsidiary corporations that control these products and their national sales to the public.

13. The "seven sisters" are interlocked with the eight largest banks of the country, as you will learn in this book. They thus control the most lucrative, profit-making product in the entire world, and through interlocking directorates they control the flow of capital to themselves to such an unbelievable degree as to shock the most sophisticated entrepreneurs of the world.

14. Russia is running out of available oil supplies in the Soviet Union. She has much oil, but so much of it is beneath the frozen tundra of the Siberian section. It is much cheaper for Russia to play up to the Arabs for their oil, and this is what they are doing now. The Soviets will need heavy oil imports in this decade of the eighties, and they have known this for years. I read about this in their papers while in Moscow four years ago. Now our papers are revealing what the Soviets need and what their game is in the Middle East.

15. The PLO cannot get Israel to give in to their demands. They will force Israel to their demands by threatening an all-out Soviet-backed Moslem holy war against the tiny state of Israel.

16. There will be an oil war (even according to ancient Biblical prophecies with Russia and the Middle East) involving many nations during the decade of the eighties. The world is rapidly at that point now. West Germany's leader Helmut Schmidt says, "We are headed for an oil war of unbelievable proportions unless something is done about oil consumption and control."

17. Gold and silver prices are rising unprecedentedly because paper currencies are falling constantly in value due to other issues. The world is in a state of fear for what is going to happen internationally.

18. NATO Forces are being beefed up for war readiness.

19. Israel believes she is going to fight the biggest war yet in the Middle East, very soon.

20. The Moslems are getting their hands on the nuclear power they have wanted for years to use against Israel.

21. It is not a question of *will we have war?* But of *when will the war break out?*

Chapter 3
The Coming Oil Showdown

Oil is black gold, and it has produced more real gold for its Middle East, African, and Indonesian owners than any other element created by God except water. Without water, 5000 years of maritime history, involving commerce, trade, and incredible amounts of moneymaking, would never have taken place. The entire history of nations and of the world would have to be rewritten, if ever written at all!

Oil has changed the entire business complexion of the world. No element has so vastly affected transportation, energy necessities for nations, business development, and the entire economies of continents like this black gold has.

Since the earliest days when a Turk and an Australian first discovered "black gold" in the Middle East, the rise of the importance of this natural element has been phenomenal.

Today as we live out the last part of the twentieth century, nations depend more on oil than on any other energy source.

Oil controls transportation, home heating, aerospace industries, food production and refinement, and even determines the amounts of secondary sources of energy that we use as electricity, since oil is used to turn the giant electroturbines that create energy for air conditioning, lighting, heating, and manufacturing. Oil affects every phase of living for modern society. Where you do not see much oil use in a country (such as in India and African countries), that country is backward, half-starving, and without industrial development and proper nutrition for its population.

God through nature gave us an abundance of this energy source. Man through greed has now gained control of this mighty power and regulates its production, refinement into other products, and retail sales in order to suit his greed and/or his political views regarding nations and their rise and fall.

Just over 50 years ago the U.S. became involved in Middle East oil when Exxon, Mobil, Gulf, and others worked their way into the oil fields, eventually producing the power they have today over America and other parts of the world.

As a result of oil's development into hundreds of by-products in the past half-century, we now have entire businesses and unbelievable fortunes made every day because of it.

Oil is involved in harvesting our crops as well as in fertilizing the fields for agricultural productivity. It is imbedded in our very way of life in America and the Western nations. Without oil we would have little transportation, industrial output, food refinement, or business operation, to say nothing of being unable to run our cars, heat and cool our homes, factories, and offices, and carry on hundreds of necessary operations to further life.

We could only live without oil if we reverted back to the primitive means of transportation we had 100 years ago.

We would have to abandon most of the sophisticated scientific discoveries of today, for many are related to this product.

The Good Old Days?

For over 5000 years mankind developed scientifically very slowly, on a graduating plateau of scientific development, until we hit the twentieth century with its oil discoveries and its mass explosion of accomplishments that changed society dramatically. Two hundred or two thousand years ago, no one would have believed what we have so marvelously achieved today in science.

One hundred years ago transportation was by the simple wheel, drawn by horses, and by water run by stream. Trains came into being using coal and steam for a newer type of transportation in Europe and the new America. In remote areas it was the dogsled and in the Orient (still today in many parts) they used the oxcart, wheel, and water transportation. China still does.

Great ships (considered great then) ferried loads of cargo by water, powered by steam.

Cooking in the home was by firewood or coal oil. Some of you remember heating up the bricks in the old woodstove and placing them in the buggy to keep your feet warm.

You may also remember that you heated the iron on the old woodstove and waited and waited for it to heat up. That is still the way it is in those parts of the world today where the use of oil-related products has yet to be implemented because of backward governments.

Hot water came from the reservoir in the old woodstove, where keeping the fire burning all night provided some warm water to wash with in the morning.

The Americans

After centuries of "wood, water, and the wheel" came the phenomenal explosion of the twentieth century with its world-revolutionizing scientific discoveries of the new generation of Americans. Most of what we call modern science today was developed by Americans. Being a Canadian myself, I am not writing from a prejudiced point of view, but very admiringly and honestly.

Americans have been first and foremost in computers, oil-drilling equipment, auto- and truck-building expertise, modern combustion engines, jet engines, supersonic planes, sophisticated communications and telecommunications, nuclear powered ocean vessels, modern conventional weapons and nuclear weaponry, the atom-splitting and atom bomb, hydrogen power, and developments for peaceful and military use of the nuclear power, Americans have done it first. They found it, used it, produced it, and then sold it and gave it away to the rest of the world.

When you join the development of oil to the American scientific explosion (including some Canadians in this scientific world), you have the greatest century of civilization and the people using it to best advantage. The Americans blended their cultural backgrounds and faith and optimism together to produce the best way of life the world has ever known.

America runs on oil today. Seventy-five percent of what North America does today depends on oil for one reason or another. Oil has invaded every industry, including lumber, food, outer space, transportation, plastics, research, laboratory science, research science, electronic industries, aerospace, sea power, and so much more. Simultaneously with the development of science came the findings of global oil lakes. One complemented the other, and here we are in the world of ever-increasing demand for oil and its benefits but a decreasing production by the people who currently control it.

The Problem Now

What is the problem now? The problem is too much consumption by the consumers of oil directly and indirectly, and a lack of production of oil by the OPEC cartel. (This is mostly Arabian oil, but it includes Venezuelan and Indonesian oil as well.)

The U.S. has diminishing supplies except for what she has discovered in the Alaskan slopes. Canada has great oil reserves in Alberta especially, and can produce most of what she needs and some for export. Mexico is just now discovering what she possesses, and the latest report is that Mexico has more oil than all of Saudi Arabia! That could be very good for the U.S. unless Europe gets to it first. Europe has the ability to negotiate quickly and diplomatically with a nation that is at odds with the U.S.

over immigration problems, etc.

In outlining the problem for the nation and for the world we face the following situations.

IRAN with her revolutionary and religious unrest has cut back considerably on production of crude oil. This has left a shortage in the world supply for some time to come.

SAUDI ARABIA, the great supplier for the United States, is cutting back now inasmuch as she is angry with the U.S. over the Israeli-Egypt peace treaty. Saudi Arabia has already cut off all aid to Egypt and its current president, Anwar Sadat.

IRAN has cut off all oil supplies to Israel, placing a heavy load on the U.S., who promised Israel aid in this area, should it be necessary, after signing the peace treaty with Egypt.

Under Iran's new revolutionary government and its aging leader Khomeini (an avowed Moslem leader), neither Israel nor the U.S. will ever get Iranian oil again. Time will tell.

Saudi Arabia has been a friend of the United States for years, inasmuch as it was American expertise that developed the oil fields in the beginning for all of these Arab countries.

Now that Saudi Arabia is angry over the Israeli-Egyptian peace accord, and blames the intervention of the United States and President Carter in particular, the Saudis have taken a hard stance against Israel and a slightly harder line against the U.S. The Crown Prince Fahd, who has been making the most of the political decisions since King Khalid has been very ill, stated that diplomatic relations with the Soviet Union could be reestablished, as he had noted the interest which the Soviets had for the Arab problem of the Palestinians in the Middle East, and he appreciated their ideas and assistance.

This is an anti-American move by the Saudis. They also stated that they would go to war (a Holy Islamic War) to return Jerusalem to the Arabs, if need be. And they have a large stockpile of American military hardware and have been thoroughly trained by American organizations on how to use it.

Not only will the Arabs continue their price hikes of a barrel of oil, as they have done many times recently, but as that continues with its consequent pricing problems for all products related to oil for the people of the world, they will then state—

Force Israel to give up the West Bank of the Jordan to the Palestinians, with total self-rule without Israeli surveillance. Force Israel to give back Jerusalem to the Arabs, or we will cut off all oil to America and those supporting America in her Pro-Israeli stance.

If the U.S. fails to do so, either in failing to try or in failing to accomplish what the Arabs want over a period of Geneva-like negotiation with Russia and others involved (including the PLO), then because of Israel's intransigency over the West Bank and Jerusalem, America and her allies will suffer overnight suffocation and strangulation of oil supplies. The Arabs will not act intelligently at that moment, but will punish the U.S. in a face-saving move against Israel.

That punishment will be drastic, dangerous, and militarily explosive. I look for war involving the United States, Russia, and Europe over the entire situation in the Middle East in this decade of the eighties.

Economic Armageddon

But first we are going to have a period (about to arrive now) that I call the ECONOMIC ARMAGEDDON.

Already in the United States we have oil and gas shortages throughout the nation at gas pumps. Even diesel fuel is in short supply, to say nothing of the long lines of empty fuel tanks waiting for gas at stations from the Eastern seaboard to California's jungle of cars and stations.

There are housing shortages due partly to oil and partly to tight-money programs aroused by the Federal Reserve Banks. As a result of that there are layoffs in supporting industries and directly related industries (lumber, steel, aluminum, tool-and-die, paint, plaster, plumbing, electrical, and so on). The unemployment lines are growing due to tight money and the oil shortage.

I still believe that the oil companies were holding back crude refinement into gasoline, so they could gouge us financially at the gas tank. They did. Have you seen their profit pictures lately? It is into the billions again, as it was in 1973, when we had shortages of gas and oil. But the oil barons made millions in profits. They have done it again. But now, added to what they are currently doing, watch for Saudi Arabia, Kuwait, and other Middle East oil-producing states to eventually cut us off!

WE ARE HEADED FOR THE ONE-CAR FAMILY IN THE UNITED STATES. We are headed for reduced pleasure, reduced necessities, and a completely reorganized financial structure of most families in the country. THERE IS NO WAY WE CAN KEEP UP THE PACE OF THE SPENDING OF THE LUCRATIVE SIXTIES!

People are changing everything from family vacation planning to family planning. I know of young married couples who have decided that children are not for them. Second cars are being sold, properties that are not being used, and some that are being used are up for sale. Buyers are getting hard to find because of the variable interest rates shoving the gross cost of the house up terribly over the years.

There is less need for appliances for new kitchens . . . we don't have the new kitchens! The same is true for plumbing for kitchens and bathrooms. Air conditioners, swimming pools, sauna baths, recreational vehicles—all sales are off. Layoffs are everywhere, with many more coming.

It is the beginning of the ECONOMIC ARMAGED-DON. Are you ready for it?

How do you get ready? Be sure to read on—I have many ideas interwoven throughout this book to help you survive it all.

Prelude to Armageddon

WE ARE HURTING NOW, BUT IN AN ELEMEN-TARY WAY COMPARED TO WHAT IS COMING SOON TO THE UNITED STATES.

WHEN WILL SAUDI ARABIA CUT IT OFF—OR THREATEN TO?

I look for continued negotiations with the Israelis and Egyptians and Americans. There will be some heavy negotiations, great disagreements, and walk-out sessions in Geneva or some other place. Great disagreements will result in heightening pressure on the U.S. as the chief negotiator in this peace endeavor. As a result, the U.S. will feel compelled for the sake of its own people to pressure Israel with threats to cut off aid, etc., should she not comply.

Most Israelis believe that it took their own blood, sons, lives, and guns to get them back to the land in 1948, and they are willing to "go it alone" now if they have to in order to keep what they have, rather than give it up. They will go down to the last man, woman, and child rather than give up Jerusalem or protection rights of the Jordan Valley. I don't blame them. They paid a terrible price for not having a home in the Second World War. Millions died. They will never forget. They also paid a terrible price in the wars in Israel since they returned. They will not give up the area of greatest importance to them—Jerusalem and the Wailing Wall. Nor will they give up their chief listening-post area on the Arab World, the West Bank of the Jordan. This area may be turned over in part to the

Arabs who are of Palestinian descent, but to turn it over and not have policing privileges or an aerial oversight of Arab actions in the Valley itself would be suicide for them.

Take the PLO's point of view of Israel. They want every Jew dead and/or out of Israel. They would sign any treaty to get the Jordan Valley. Would they keep their part of the treaty? Certainly not. They are avowed killers of Israel and would do anything to get them out. They would use Soviet-supplied military hardware, and the Israelis know this. So do I, having been with my wife on both sides of the situation many times, visiting with them both, somewhat sympathizing with them.

We have Palestinian friends and Israeli friends of long standing. It is a terrible shame and tragedy that peace cannot be worked out between them. But I believe that it cannot be for now. The hatred is too deep at present.

We are feeling this hatred here in the U.S. We are going to feel it even more. They are going to make us feel it. Many people are already feeling it in their pocketbooks, their job security, and their lifestyles. Many more of us are going to feel it where it will hurt the most—right in the breadbox! But hopefully not to the extent that our sons will be fighting again on foreign soil! We will cover that in the next chapter.

A mass migration of people in the U.S. from the north to the south is happening now. They feel they can get a job there, and even if they cannot, they can grow a garden and survive what is going to happen. They can live without winter heating fuel, and thus live cheaper with respect to both heating and clothing.

For the time being, it will all be dialogue and debate over the Israeli situation. President Sadat could be murdered— God forbid! They have a price on his head.

Shortages will appear all across the country—crippling shortages in some areas. There will be shortages of dollars to spend, shortages of products to buy, shortages of tourists everywhere. There will be shortages of fuel for heating and driving and shortages of luxuries and many necessities.

My Advice

STOCK UP NOW. Buy extra canned food and put them away. The day is coming. Buy dehydrated and freeze-dried foods and store them. They take up much less room than water-preserved foods and last much longer—up to 10 and 15 years in some cases.

SECURE SOME BOTTLED WATER IN YOUR HOUSE. Get extra everything. Especially get candles and matches and place them where you remember they are and out of the reach of children!

Get some extra tires and extra gas, stored now safely. Also, change your car to a smaller one. Get additional prescriptions; buy first-aid equipment for your family; consider a retreat out of where you live to the country. Can you afford to lease a retreat and move there now? If so, by all means do it. (See my book *How to Survive the Money Crash,* by Harvest House Publishers, Irvine, California. Ask for it in your local bookstore. It tells the whole story of what to have, where to live, and what to get NOW. Hundreds of thousands have this book. You need it.)

Get yourself a retreat safely tucked away from the large city. Stock it well with food, water, safety items, fuel, and all kitchen and bathroom necessities.

Stay away from earthquake faults and tornado and hurricane paths when looking for a retreat, and especially stay away from areas where there could be crossfire amid differing nationalities blaming one another for the trouble.

Do not broadcast what you have or where you would go in a time of trouble. Keep things to yourself and try to get your adult children to do the same. It may be best to tell them nothing!

When the economic Armageddon really strikes, you will have plenty of warning. The newspapers will shout the headlines: WAR WITH THE ARABS COMING SOON. TV and radio will tell the heartbreaking story of the Arabs turning the pressure on us to get what they want and cannot get themselves from Israel.

There may be a time of peaceful negotiations and promises from all sides but don't count on it. We will not force Israel into anything. The Israelis will do little budging on any issue of any substance. The United States will find herself helplessly adrift in the middle of a sea of hatred, resentment, and distrust in the Middle East, with the Soviets sitting at the same table, constantly irritating the Arabs and producing a hard-line stance by the Arabs in every point.

The Arabs will not lose face. They want the city of Jerusalem. They want the West Bank in Palestinian hands completely. They will not stop short on one of these issues. Oil will be used as a weapon!

Should America not deliver, and we will not, the Arabs will then storm out (some of the hotheads), while others will quietly smile and simply state to the negotiators that they have 90 days (or so) to produce results as demanded, or else all oil will be phased out completely, until Israel meets the Arabs' demands.

THIS WILL TOPPLE THE STOCK MARKET OVERNIGHT.

Businesses will go bankrupt, and I am talking about big business that will take advantage of the bankruptcy act to save their hidden assets, etc.

CRITICAL SHORTAGES OF EVERY PRODUCT YOU CAN IMAGINE WILL OCCUR IMMEDIATELY. PANIC BUYING WILL EMPTY SHELVES EVERYWHERE.

Suicides and mental disorders will increase everywhere as despair engulfs a generation of Americans who did not live through the Great Depression and have been raised on false ideas of self expression and nondiscipline. They will not be able to handle defeat, lessening of necessities, and changing lifestyles so severe as to be indescribable at this point.

Look for an ECONOMIC ARMAGEDDON that will increase crime staggering. Black-market selling and buying of all products will produce a new level of economics.

During the unbelievable unemployment that will quickly develop, the government will have to turn on the presses of the Federal Reserve System incredulously in order to keep the complete depression-collapse from happening overnight! This runaway inflation of currency and credit will produce the depression just a little later, but the government will not be able to stop it.

People who at this time have money in the bank could lose it. Banks will suddenly close, as they did in 1929. Millions will lose billions!

As result of unemployment (as a direct result of oil cutoffs) thousands will give up their mortgages on cars and homes and will be unable to pay their monthly installments on appliances, second homes, or extra luxuries. *It will be all they can do to keep body and soul and family together.*

The Inevitable

THIS IS ECONOMIC ARMAGEDDON. It is not a prediction based on mere assumption. This is not a prophecy of doom and gloom without foundation.

I know the Arabs. I understand the State of Israel, having been there nearly two dozen times. We all know the power of oil and who controls it. We are in for everything in this chapter and more!

There is nothing you can do to stop this, but you can start NOW to protect your family from what is coming soon!

Do not put off what you know you can do. Do it now.

Buy gold coins—preferably the South African Krugerrand and the new Canadian Maple Leaf coin—and save them till the rainy day. The time will come when dollar bills will be worthless. If you hold gold then, you will be saved from disaster, safe from entire loss, and in a position to feed yourself and your family.

Silver coins minted in the U.S. up to and including the year 1964 are equally good for buying food and necessities in the tough times surely coming soon. More on this later.

Europeans will be the first ones to tell us, "CUT BACK ON YOUR OIL CONSUMPTION OR WE'LL JOIN THE ARABS OVER THE MIDEAST SITUATION."

Europeans believe we live too high anyway. They have a built-in desire to live like us, and there is some jealousy. Many will admit that they would like to have the American dream, but know it is impossible. This will give their leaders the chance to break with the U.S. over the oil-consumption questions. They will not hesitate to do so, imposing even worse conditions on us.

Japan and China will remain quiet to it all, secretly making deals to buy the extra gas and oil available from the Arab oil producers. The Arabs will lose very little by not selling to the U.S. Many buyers are out there. The thought of oil being used as the ultimate weapon is not new. The threats keep coming.

The extremely volatile situation of the Middle East is about to blow up in our faces painfully and without remedy. Israel will not give in. The Arabs will not give up. The coming of the oil war is just a matter of time.

With U.S. Embassies under attack in many Moslem countries, beginning with the Iranians taking the American hostages, no one seriously doubts that we are headed for great bloodshed.

Our problems with the Shah of Iran and the revolutionary government of Iran only further complicates U.S. negotiations concerning Israel. The Middle East is a fast-growing, daily compounding dilemma poised as a snake to strike America at any moment.

Chapter 4
Worse Than World War Two

Picture the scene in your imagination.

Israel is beseiged politically by the U.S. and most countries of the world to give up Jerusalem and the West Bank in order to let the oil flow again to the needy nations of the world.

But Israel is adamantly opposed, and nations sever their diplomatic relations with Tel Aviv and Jerusalem immediately. If Israel ever saw herself exiled from the world, it will be then.

Israel will be on total military alert, for PLO sabotage will have increased terrifyingly. It is starting now.

Every night murders of Israeli citizens will take place by the Yasser Arafat followers, financed by Libya and other Arab States and armed by the Soviets. Diplomats from every nation will be leaving Israel.

The United Nations will expel Israel from membership. One by one, European nations from the east and west blocs will leave Israel, until only a few diehards like Holland, England, and maybe Scotland will remain, along with the United States.

Canada may stay with the U.S. or may declare neutrality. Being somewhat self-sufficient in oil and natural resources, Canada can feel easy about ignoring the situation or helping Israel.

China, in return for U.S. leadership in her oil exploration and development, will aid the U.S. in the oil squeeze.

Mexico will see a new day dawn for Mexican-American relationships and will sell crude oil in exchange for

American food. A new president will negotiate that deal and swing into the White House on that platform!

Canada will help the United States with natural resources and oil (along with water) in return for technology to develop outer areas heavily laden with goodies from mother nature, yet untouched.

The military machine will grind 168 hours a week in the country. Everything will be in a state of readiness for an international showdown called WAR.

The Bold Soviets

Detente will be set aside with the Soviet Union.

The Russians will be talking hard, and the cold war will be on in earnest. The Soviets feel they have the superior position in weapons and men. They will flaunt SALT in our faces and laugh at our admitted compliance and readily reveal that they duped us.

MAD—Mutual Assured Destruction—has kept the two major nations from fighting until this moment. This was the theory devised by both—that to fight each other meant annihilation of both sides.

But now that is all off. The Soviets have "hardened" their necessary industries, meaning that they have secretly sandbagged and built protective coverings over all industries and diversified their locations out of the big industrial cities. Much of their production is now underground, to the chagrin of the U.S.

They have a superior army, navy, and air force, backed by long-range missiles and roving nuclear-powered submarines capable of knocking out every major American city in one hour with multiple-entry warheaded missiles and major new weapons.

Their Backfire bombers are powerful and outfly the U.S., since we cut back on development of the sophisticated B-1 Bomber under President Carter, and the neutron bomb was shelved (which would have given us an edge on them, or at least parity with their offensive weapons).

The Soviets are cocky and the Arab anger will boil. The weaknesses of the United States in pressuring Israel into acquiescing over the West Bank and Jerusalem will be aired in the world press. U.S. stock will fall in world opinion. She has a weak President and congress, they will say.

Already hurting over the oil cutback of Iran and other Arab states, the U.S. by this time will be virtually paranoid that the Arabs will use their trump card.

But the card will be played. "FORCE ISRAEL INTO COMPLIANCE WITH PLO AND ARAB DEMANDS, OR YOUR OIL WILL BE PHASED OUT BEGINNING IN 30 DAYS. YOU HAVE 90 DAYS TO CONVINCE ISRAEL OF HER WORLD RESPONSIBILITY."

At that time, as indicated in the preceding chapter, panic will hit the streets of North America. All that I suggested will happen when the Saudis deliver the deathblow.

The psychology of what is going to take place in those 30 to 60 days will hit the American people like a fatal blow beneath the belt.

Mass movements of Soviet troops, plus war machinery and supplies, will be airlifted to parts of the Middle East. Damascus will see unprecedented Soviet powers moving in, just a few short miles from the Israeli border. I personally have already been arrested for filming Soviet missiles aimed at Israeli positions, just outside Damascus! It was a great experience. I was militarily arrested and within three hours released with apologies. I did not know the missiles were there, and had been invited by the Syrian government to film Damascus. I caught the missiles in the telephoto lens. Far be it from me to turn down a good thing!

While under military arrest for a while, I saw that the military controls the civilian government in Syria completely. It is a military rule.

While Damascus will swell with Soviet military advisors and intelligence, Amman in Jordan (under King Hussein) will be the very same! You can look for King Hussein (a moderate in Mideast affairs thus far) to join the militants against Israel, especially if he knows the Russians are behind the Arab effort, and not just the other Arabs pushing at Israel again. He knows this will be a fully mechanized, military push of a nuclear nature against the hated Israeli nation next to him.

Remember, King Hussein lived in East Jerusalem in a beautiful, palace-like home prior to 1967, when the Israeli government took over. The King wants Jerusalem back under his jurisdiction. And, though he has been relatively friendly to Israel during the decade of the seventies, he resents their presence and wants his city back.

Jordanian soil will bristle with Soviets, armor, and the PLO awaiting the world to attack the Holy City again.

Lebanon will probably join the attack, as the moderates will have been forced to succumb to the militant members of the PLO in that formerly Christian country. Israel will be surrounded on the north by Lebanon, on the east by Syria and Jordan, on the south by Saudi Arabia, and on the west by the largest Soviet fleet in any water—floating menacingly in the Mediterranean Sea, with the U.S. fleet sailing protectively in the distance.

The Mideast Military Might

The latest statistics on military might in the Middle East with the Moslem armies indicate formidable strength, along with the mighty power of the Soviets to back them up with men and machinery more sophisticated than they have ever used before.

In Saudi Arabia there are 45,000 American-trained men in the army. Jordan has 61,000 men, Syria has 200,000 men; Turkey has 390,000 men; Iraq commands 180,000 men; Iran has over 285,000; the army of Kuwait is 10,500; Qater, 3,500; United Arab Emirates, 23,500; Oman has 16,200; South Yemen has 36,000; North Yemen has 19,000; if you include others in the area sympathetic to the cause (apart from Egypt), you have the Sudan with, 50,000; Ethiopia, with 90,000; Somalia, with 50,000; Libya, with 200,000; Afghanistan, with 100,000; and Pakistan, with 400,000. This presents a tremendous united army against Israel, to fight along with the superior Soviet strength pouring in at that time.

Israel keeps a standing army of 138,000 highly skilled fighting men armed to the teeth with the best equipment America could provide.

There is also no doubt that Israel has nuclear-powered missiles, and will use them against this overwhelming enemy if it should become necessary. I believe it will become necessary.

You have to know that Israel will do anything it has to do to protect itself from this enemy. The Jews have everything to lose if they compromise and fail. They are willing to give the very best of what they possess in order to win. Can they possibly win with such a fierce enemy possessing such tremendous odds? That is the question.

Who will help Israel at this time? Is there a nation on earth that would offer a helping hand in this moment of finality? Is there one member of the U.N. that would break ranks with the majority and take a stand to help this infant Middle East power and stave off her annihilation? Unless someone somewhere helps, it will mean annihilation for sure. Even if the Arabs did not possess nuclear power themselves, which they do, the Soviets have all they need.

Half of all the world's oil is shipped from the Strait of Hormuz, between Pakistan and Oman. If all these nations turn against the United States, as I am predicting they will, we will have little left as an option but to fight against them, or else give in to them and join the battle AGAINST ISRAEL OURSELVES in order to get our oil.

THAT WILL NEVER HAPPEN. We will never give in and fight Israel. This nation will never join the Arabs in this battle. We would never join the Soviets in squashing the Israeli ant in the Middle East. Our Judeo-Christian roots are too entwined.

It has been said that we are through fighting our Vietnams. That is so. We will probably never fight that type of war again. But you must remember that this was a war for *someone else*. This will be a war for *us and our own interests*.

We need oil. We will fight for it.

We have an inherited relationship with Israel that this nation will never turn its back on. Whether some like it or not, part of America is its strong Jewish-American population. They work in every avenue of endeavor in this country, and from top to bottom they are in every walk of life and every business effort. We have Jews in the Senate and in the House of Representatives, and for the most part Jews are the most vociferous of the President's cabinet.

There will be a backlash among some Americans, but this country will go to war, with its men on foreign soil, to protect Israel from the Arabs and the Soviets.

The United States will accept the declaration of war against Israel as a declaration of war against the U.S., and our country will mobilize.

Oil will come from our neighbors to the north and the south. Both have enough for all three of us, in addition to that we will utilize our own supplies internally. We will make it.

If you believe that this book has been full of doom and gloom for Americans and Israelis, let me make the next statement firm and solid, loud and clear.

THIS IS A WAR WE ARE GOING TO WIN. THE SOVIETS WILL BE DEFEATED ONCE-AND-FOR-ALL. THEY WILL BE PULVERIZED AND AMERICA WILL STAND UNDEFEATED, THOUGH BLEEDING BADLY, BUT NOT FATALLY. THE ARABS WILL BE COMPLETELY NEUTRALIZED AND PARALYZED ONCE-AND-FOR-ALL. THEY WILL NEVER FIGHT ISRAEL AGAIN. THEY WILL NOT BE DESTROYED, BUT WILL BE MILITARILY DEFEATED FOREVER. RUSSIAN COMMUNISM WILL BE DEFEATED. THE EASTERN NATIONS OF THE WARSAW PACT ARMIES (SOVIET CONTROLLED) WILL NEVER FIGHT AGAIN, AND THOSE NATIONS WILL BE GREATLY DESTROYED BY THEIR AMERICAN ENEMY.

Questions and Answers

Questions immediately appear on the horizon of our minds. How will the U.S. defeat the Russians so thoroughly? How badly will the United States bleed in this war? How many will die? Will the Soviets use nuclear powers against the mainland United States? Will we use ours against them? How will Israel survive the nuclear onslaught? How do we really know that Russian forces will join the Arabs in this all-out effort against Israel? What documentation is there for such ominous assumptions?

For part of this answer let me relate to you a conversation I had with the late former Prime Minister of Israel, Mr. David Ben-Gurion, in his kibbutz one day. He was the "Moses" of modern Israel.

After welcoming me as a journalist and television producer, we talked about his memoirs and life as Prime Minister. Ben-Gurion said:

"Clark, I have lived through four wars here and seen this tiny nation come from nothing to what it is today. I fought and I led men into death for this soil, and the greatest moment I had as Prime Minister was when we took Jerusalem after 1900 years of being exiled from our own land." He paused. "But we took it, and we will never give up Jerusalem again until the last man and woman is dead defending it. No matter what the cost, we will never give it up until the last Jew is dead. That's how all our people feel."

He went on to describe how he and the nation felt upon the taking of Jerusalem and how they "sanctified it for three days from Gentile feet" after taking it. No one but Jews could come to the city for three days. The nation wept. Jews danced. The Prime Minister thanked God. Historic Israel was together on home soil after two millenniums.

"Then I realized that we would fight another war in this land—bigger and bloodier than any before it. We are going to be invaded by Russia and the Arabs soon." He watched for my reaction and went on. "I feel it in my bones, and, being a Polish Jew, I know how Russians think in their hierarchy. They want the minerals of the Dead Sea and the oil of the Middle East. But more than that, Clark, they want the geographical position of Israel in the Middle East for themselves."

I asked what he meant. Oil and minerals were plain to me, but not this last statement.

"Look at the map with me." We did. We both took a look at his map of the Middle East, with Russia looming far above it—above Asia.

"As you can see, Clark, the little State of Israel is a tiny bridge to three continents. We are a bridge to Asia on the East, Europe on the North, and Africa on the South. Whoever controls this tiny strip of land has access to three major continents, and this is the center of the earth.

"You can go down the Red Sea to the Indian Ocean from our ports and into the Mediterranean Sea to Europe and America from our ports. You have it all."

"The Russians *want* it all. They will make friends with the Arabs and get a promise of their oil, which they will desperately need themselves fairly soon. In addition to commitments from the Arabs, they will get a fair chunk of this land for their own selfish interests internationally."

I asked Ben-Gurion if he had ever studied anything about a Russian invasion of the Middle East—Israel in particular—from the Bible's prophecies.

He answered no, but was interested to know if anything was there.

I proceeded to explain the following Biblical prophecy given by one of his illustrious Jewish Prophets, Ezekiel, and what Ezekial had to say about the invasion from the North. Here is the prediction, with my clarifications included for your understanding of what the original text presents, as I presented it to the Prime Minister of Israel.

> *And the word of the Lord came unto me, saying, son of man, set thy face against Gog, the land of Magog (Russia), the Chief Prince of Meshech (Moscow) and Tubal (Tubolsk), and prophesy against him, and saith the Lord God, behold, I am against thee, O Gog, The Chief Prince of Meshech and Tubal; and I will turn thee back, and put hooks into thy jaws, and I will bring thee forth, and all thine army, horses and horsemen, all of them clothed with all sorts of armor, even a great company with bucklers and shields, all of them handling swords: Persia, Ethiopia, and Libya with them, all of them with shield and helmet; Gomer and all his bands; the House of Togarmah of the North Quarters, and all his bands; and many people with thee (Ezekiel 38: 1-6).*

Persia is today's Middle Eastern countries just east of Israel, including Syria, Jordan, Iraq, Iran, Afghanistan, Pakistan, Qatar, Kuwait, United Arab Emirates, Oman, South and North Yemen, Saudi Arabia, and Lebanon.

This was the area of ancient Persia. Gomer was the original Gomerites who settled around the areas of Germany, Poland, and some of the Eastern Slavic countries. They now make up the Warsaw Pact Nations, and their armies will march with the Soviets. Togarmah to the original Jew (and still today for those who know their ancient geography) was Asia Minor, or today's Turkey. In that statement you have *all the Moslem nations, including those of Africa.*

> *After many days thou shalt be visited: in the latter years thou shalt come into the land that is brought back from the sword, and is gathered out of many people, against the mountains of Israel, which have always been waste; but is brought forth out of the nations, and they shall dwell safely all of them (Ezekiel 38:8)*

The timing of the fulfillment of this prophecy would have to be, as the Prophet said, in the *latter* years, for Israel had to come home after being dispersed to many nations and many people. Also, the use of the word "nations" does not refer to the ancient Babylonian captivity which the nation of Israel went into in 586 B.C. for 70 years, for this prophecy was written after that captivity, when the Jews were back in Palestine (until A.D. 70, when they were dispersed everywhere by the Roman army). It was not until then that they entered into many nations. Therefore this prophecy could not have been fulfilled before A.D. 70 and could not be fulfilled until after the Jews came back to the land in 1948. It has never been fulfilled in either ancient or modern history, and, therefore it must be a future, yet-unfulfilled edict of God for Israel. It eventually will involve all Moslems in a Holy War against Israel, and includes a country called MAGOG.

Historically, Jews relate Magog to be a grandson of

Noah, who went north of the Mountains of Ararat and inhabited what we today call Russia. They called this the land of the Magogites and later the land of the Roshites ("Russians"), now called Soviets.

I further shared with the Prime Minister (and with many others everywhere I go) that when Russia attacks she will attack Israel with all of Persia by her side. Persian territory of the past covers *all* the Arab nations of today.

The words "in the latter years" also require the fulfillment to be at a time much later than the writing of this book of Ezekiel, written in the fifth century B.C.

When Israel came back from Babylonian captivity, she came back from *one* nation's captivity—not many nations. And besides, this prophecy was given after that period of time.

It is a prophecy for *our* times, I told the Prime Minister. The prophecy goes on to say—

Thou shalt ascend and come like a storm; thou shalt be like a cloud to cover the land, thou and all thy bands, and many people with thee. . . . Thou shalt say, I will go up to the land of unwalled village; I will go to them that are at rest, that dwell safely, all of them dwelling without walls, and having neither bars nor gates, to take a spoil [oil?] and to take a prey; to turn thine hand upon the desolate places that are now inhabited, and upon the people that are gathered out of the nations, which have gotten cattle and goods, that dwell in the midst of the land. . . . Thou shalt come from thy place out of the north parts. . . and thou shalt come up against My people of Israel. . . . It shall be in the latter days, and I will bring thee against My land, that the heathen may know Me, when I shall be sanctified in thee, O Gog, before their eyes. . . . And it shall come to pass at the same time when Gog shall come against the land of Israel, saith the Lord God, that My fury shall come up in My face. . . . And I will call for a sword against him throughout all My mountains saith the Lord God; every man's sword shall be against his brother. And I will plead against him with pestilence and with blood; and I will rain upon him, and upon his bands, and upon the many people that are with him, an overglowing rain, and great hailstones, fire, and brimstone. Thus will I magnify Myself, and sanctify myself; and I will be known in the eyes of many nations, and they shall know that I am the Lord. (Ezekiel 38:9-23).

Israel's Ally

Interestingly enough, this prophecy indicated to me and to the Prime Minister that God would have to call on *someone* to have a sword handy with which to fight the aggressors. That sword would have to be the *sword of an ally to Israel* against the opposing forces.

There is only one nation on earth unilaterally committed to helping Israel today, and that nation is the United States of America.

Whether you believe in an ancient Jewish prophecy or not, the facts do support the timing and immensity of the prophecy. Of course the credibility of the Prophet Ezekiel is so far impeccable.

He did predict in chapters 36 and 37 that the Jews would return to their native land after a long period of being away.

They *were* away a long time. They *did* come home from many nations. He was right on that score. Whether we are religious or not, we must give the Prophet his due respect. Everything he said about the Jews, the Russians, and the Arabs is coming to pass.

If everything else is correct and every fact of modern life today seems to back up his statements, then we can look for all hell to break loose soon in the Middle East, affecting the entire Western world. Millions in the Jewish and

Christian world believe this prophecy.

It is entirely possible that Egypt will refrain from entering this war. She is not involved by name in the ancient prophecy at all. Did this leave room for the Israeli-Egyptian peace accord of 1979 under President Carter's direction?

Interestingly enough, neither in the prophecy of Daniel (11:40-45) nor in the amazing prophecy of Ezekiel is Egypt mentioned as fighting with the other Moslems or Arabs against Israel. As a matter of fact, the prophecies are silent on Egypt at this time with respect to her fighting at all.

If the only genuine uniting principle finally bringing all the Moslem countries together to fight Israel is the taking of the Holy City (provoked by the PLO for their greater desires), the only genuine principle that would make the United States fight another war is the loss of its energy source—oil from the Middle East. That could motivate the man on the street to fight. We will never fight another Korea or Vietnam, but we would fight for the things we want. If that means fighting overseas on foreign soil, then we will have the will both in the government and in the people to do so readily.

There will certainly be a backlash of "Jew-haters" who will say, "Let them fight their own war." There have always been that type.

Others will march on Washington to enforce their opinion that we should be neutral (like Canada perhaps will be) and that for our own good we should unofficially join the Arab movement. "Look what being on the side of the State of Israel is doing to us!" This latter movement will be big, but unable to budge the government and thus the majority of the people from the position of helping Israel. America has always had the fatherly image and compassion to help the underdog. This emotion will surface, along with other motivations to fight.

According to the prophecy, Russia (the Soviets) will

move down through Turkey (who will be an ally) into Syria and Lebanon and Jordan, and will form a front line of attack in these nations touching Israel.

Backup forces will be in Saudi Arabia, Iraq, Iran, and around the Persian Gulf to keep the U.S. from coming in the back door of the Persian Gulf to get the oil or to attack the enemy.

This will all take time, though not as much as you might think. Some moves will be hidden, and others most evident, as a trial balloon to pressure the United States into giving in, thereby saving themselves the terrible ravages of war.

I can see the Arabs even promising the U.S. oil—now that she has tried to pressure the State of Israel into giving up the West Bank and Jerusalem—if the U.S. will stay out of the war completely. But this will simply be a trick to keep us neutral. Some will want to believe and stay out and "see if they will keep their word."

There will be a great temptation to do so. Forces within the U.S. will divide over this issue more than over any issue in American history. Nations everywhere will tell us to stay out. "You have done your part in pressuring and negotiating." Millions of Americans, at this promise of oil for staying out, will rise up and protest as doves against the hawks.

First Strike?

Only if the United States has its back up against the wall will it strike first in this war. Given the opportunity (and they will have it) the Israelis *will* strike first, for often the best defense is to take the offense. Strike while the enemy is getting ready and not fully prepared. Israeli action will have to be swift and paralyzing in order to keep from being wiped off the face of the map immediately.

Should Israel deploy nuclear weapons with precision, which they could and would in a situation like this, devastating damage could be inflicted on the Soviets and

Arabs in spite of their formidable numbers and weaponry.

With the United States' nuclear fleets in the Mediterranean Sea and Indian Ocean, along with ground forces already in Israel and perhaps even stationed in Egypt or in the Sinai (in addition to the peace-keeping forces that will be there soon), we could already be in a state-of-war readiness with Israel, ready to strike first at the Soviet's homeland with missiles from this Mideast area, and of course also from land-based missile sites in the United States and from nuclear ships and submarines.

If this war leads to an ALL-OUT CONFRONTATION OF THE SUPERPOWERS IN NUCLEAR DESTRUCTION, then the United States could and would do their best to wipe out the enemies' ability to wipe us out first.

We must also remember that our forces in Western Europe with NATO will be in a state of war readiness along with other NATO forces, who by then will know that if Russia gets the Mideast oil she could well starve her European enemies out (as well as America).

Europe will join this war on the same side as the United States, but only *after* she is sure that a Soviet win would cripple Western Europe's industries and sovereignties. When the other NATO forces understand that a Russian win brings Russian-type Communist power to all of Europe, then they will rise up and do battle alongside the United States. The best the United States and Europe and Israel could hope for would be to strike first and diminish the enemy's ability to counter-strike.

The War Losses

We have to realize that the Soviets will be able to unleash some terrible nuclear power against us from roving nuclear-powered and nuclear-armed submarines in the Atlantic and Pacific Oceans, to say nothing about what the Soviets have hidden in Cuba ready for death and destruction on our own mainland.

There is no way, banning a miracle from heaven, that

the United States, Europe, and Israel will not be seriously injured in the retaliation strike from the enemy. I do not look for miracles at this time in this way.

Realistically, we know that Europe could lose at least one quarter of its population and have tragic destruction inflicted on its industrial sights, with nuclear fallout so serious as to endanger its agricultural ability for years. Certainly 50 million Western Europeans could die in this way, to say nothing of the 255 million Russians and 105 million Eastern Europeans that will receive the impact of the American, NATO and Israeli nuclear weapons, with the latter being more local in the Middle East, and America and Europe aiming at all of Eastern Europe and the missile bases of the entire Soviet Union and its satellites.

Not all of Russia or her allies will be destroyed, but they can count on at least 25 percent or more in spite of an excellent civil-defense program. But they may not have time to activate this program should their enemy decide to strike first. The Soviets do not think we would ever do this.

They have developed a very effective civil-defense program. We have developed nothing. It is a farce in this country, and we have our leaders to blame. Not even the President has a plan for the people.

It is most reasonable to assume, unfortunately, that even with a strike-first capacity, plus will and action by America, we could lose between 10 and 50 million Americans off the face of the earth in this next war! That is the reason for this book.

That is horrible, we all realize. But it seems inevitable, the way the world is moving now and the way oil is becoming the number one problem. Do you actually doubt this in your heart? Remember Tehran!

How does one survive such severe, unprecedented devastation? Is there anything we can do now to prevent this war? Yes, there is, as far as America is concerned.

Prophecy is prophecy. It will be fulfilled, but we do not have to be involved, providing we do certain things now.

Those things will be covered in the next chapter.

In case you feel the above case is not substantiated, and that Russia and the Arabs are not planning the above, then the following statements, facts, and statistics may help to convince you.

The Facts and Statistics

Lenin, the father of modern-day Russian Communism, stated:

"We are living not merely in a state but in a system of states, and it is inconceivable that the Soviet Republic should continue to exist for a longer period of time side by side with imperialist states. Ultimately, one or the other must conquer."

More recently Breshnev said:

"We must never forget that the mission that falls to the Communist Party is the grandiose, complex mission of revolutionary transformation of the entire world society."

Soviet Defense Spending: *Monthly Economic Letter,* **August 1979, Citibank Economic Department, New York City.**

"Western estimates tend to place Soviet defense expenditures at about 12-15% of total GNP, a significantly greater share than that of other major industrialized nations, including the U.S. When broken down . . . Soviet military investment has been about 75% greater than that of the U.S. since 1975. The Soviets spent significantly greater amounts on ICBMs and on land forces and spent less on strategic bombers and on tactical air forces (yet they have the Backfire supersonic bomber and we don't have the B1.) It is clear that the Soviets have continued to expand their arsenal, in spite of very high costs to the non-military sectors of their economy. . . . What all this means is that the old assumptions of the obvious U.S. military superiority are no longer valid."

New Soviet Missile-Immune Tank: *London Times,* **July 1979.**

"The Soviet Union is developing a new tank that could seriously undermine the present defense strategy of the NATO forces protecting the West. To counter the overwhelming Soviet numerical superiority in tanks, NATO is equipping its forces with a new generation of antitank missiles. But the Soviet tank, designated the T-80, will be immune to them, reports claim.

"Prototypes of the T-80 exist and have already undergone field trials. If the reports are accurate, and if the Russians follow their normal development pace, the T-80 will be in service in Eastern Europe by the early '80's!

"Some data about the T-80 seems speculative, but the crucial point is that the Russians have apparently developed a type of composite armor consisting of a honeycomb of steel, ceramics, and aluminum.

"This will provide the T-80 with three times the protection of conventional steel armor, yet the tank will weigh little more.

"Since 1970 the Soviets have increased their European forces by more than 100,000 men and their tank inventory by 40%. They have deployed the modern Backfire Bomber (not covered in Carter's new SALT II treaty) and they have deployed the SS-20, a mobile, multiple-warhead missile with a range of 4,000 kilometers. The latest Warsaw Pact exercises are predicated on beating NATO to the draw with nuclear weapons. The SS-20 would be particularly effective in taking out NATO ports and airfields to hurt reinforcement capability and leave the Soviets with a massive conventional advantage."

A New USSR Bomber Better Than Their Backfire: *Defense and Foreign Affairs Daily,* **February 6, 1978, Washington, D.C.**

"U.S. Defense Secretary Brown told Congress the U.S. was expecting the Soviet Union to fly the first prototype of a new heavy bomber in the near future. The aircraft would be different from and presumably larger than the Backfire.

The news came only 2 days after the U.S. Senate declined to appropriate further funds for the development of a further two B-1 prototypes.''

General Keegan Issues Warning.

''The Soviets have deployed and developed the most intensive system of nuclear shelter for its military leadership, its civilian leadership, its industrial factory workers, and its civilian population ever deployed or built in history. The result is, if they attacked the United States about 160,000,000 Americans would die, and probably no more than 5,000,000 Russians.''

Soviet Satellite Data Shocks Carter: *Defense and Foreign Affairs Daily,* **May, 1979.**

''News that the Soviet Union has, for some time, been preparing a satellite-killing capability reportedly came as a shock recently to the U.S. Administration. According to reliable sources, Carter was appalled to learn how the USSR had progressed in the relevant technology. He ordered a thorough investigation on the Soviet killer systems.

''The U.S. has little to equip itself with a similar system.

''A Soviet ability to kill U.S. vehicles translates into a Soviet capability of knocking out, or at least blinding, U.S. early-warning vehicles. Such satellites are in orbit to watch for ICBM launches. They could be rendered useless.''

3 Years Left? *The Kiplinger Letter,* **May, 1979.**

''By 1981 or 1982 Russia would have superiority over the U.S. That's what the U.S. intelligence people foresee. The Soviets would have a missile strength so deep they could retaliate even after a missile strike by the U.S. They could hit us a second time!

''Probably they wouldn't need to. The mere threat of another blow might do the trick. In fact, the knowledge of mighty red power could be sufficient to make the U.S. knuckle under . . . without a fight.''

War Is Coming: *Defense and Foreign Affairs Daily,* **May, 1979.**

"Everybody talks about war, but nobody seems to do much about it. Except hasten it. And there does seem to be a growing consensus, largely reflected in the ongoing research which the Digest and its sister publications undertake, that major war is not far distant.

"Two major camps of the population in the West take divergent views. One group is dedicated to appeasement and unilateral disarmament, or partial disarmament, ignoring the fundamental physics which say that when vacuums are created something rushes in to fill the void. The other group has a "chicken little" mentality which notes that the sky has fallen or, to mix metaphors, cries wolf. But there is a war coming! To deny it would be to deny man's historical cycles and proclivities; like denying that the majority of mankind will go to sleep tonight and wake on the morrow. The question is what to do about this war in the years before it happens. To minimize its effect might be one approach, through reducing unhealthy jugular-like imbalanced dependencies on oil. In such an approach, the search for alternative fuels is an imperative. The superpowers are meanwhile plodding along a collision course, and their collective attitude towards the problem seems to be to look to anything but reality. It seems more like a collision course."

The Russian Timetable: *Defense and Foreign Affairs Daily,* **May, 1979.**

"Soviet President Leonid Brezhnev informed members of his Politburo that, 'We Communists have got to string along with the capitalists for a while. We need their credits, their technology and their agriculture. But we are going to continue a massive military build-up, and by the middle 1980's we will be in a position to return to a much more aggressive foreign policy designed to gain the upper hand in our relationship with the West.' "

Soviet Missiles Outclass Those of the U.S.: *UPI, London,* **May, 1979.**

"The U.S. could fire more than twice as many nuclear warheads as the Soviets in case of war, but Russia's atomic weapons pack a greater punch, the International Institute for Strategic Studies says. The institute, an independent international center for information and research on problems of the security of nations and defense and control in a nuclear age, also said the military balance in Europe is moving steadily against the West. The Soviet's individual warheads have significantly higher yields than the U.S. And on the sea there is litle doubt that the Soviet naval forces now pose a threat to NATO."

French Say Red Attack More Possible. *UPI, Paris,* **May, 1979.**

"French military authorities say Soviet bloc countries have reached such strength in Europe that a surprise attack by the Warsaw Pact is more and more possible. The Soviet command may now believe that the balance of forces in Europe has decisively tipped in its favor.

"Russia has a 3 to 1 advantage in the field of airborne and land forces, due to Western powers' slack defense efforts."

The Bear at the Backdoor: *New Hampshire Union Leader,* **May, 1979.**

"A former top commander of the NATO forces has warned that Russia has a grand design of domination, aimed at outflanking Europe at sea, taking control of oil supplies, dominating the sea routes in the Indian Ocean and Atlantic, gaining dominance of Western Europe and then dictating to the United States.

"The grim warning has come from General Sir Walter Walker, NATO commander-in-chief, Allied Forces Northern Europe from 1969 to 1972. He set out a grim picture of Soviet designs and Western failings in a book entitled THE BEAR AT THE BACKDOOR, just published in London. General Walker depicts the likely scenario of

Soviet blitzkreig in Europe, if Moscow decided on outright aggression. It goes like this.

"At 5 PM on a Friday evening, when NATO forces have stood for the weekend, a combined Soviet airborne and naval assault under the guise of maneuvers would be launched against Denmark, the "cork" in the Baltic Sea. It would be met by the Danish army, which is about half of the size of the New York City Police Dept.

"The assault would aim at occupying the northern tip of Norway and Denmark, which dominate the Soviet sea passage to the Indian Ocean.

"Simultaneously, on the Central Front across the North German Plain, the Warsaw Pact forces would crunch their way forward, with overwhelming tank and air forces at 70 miles a day. The speed would be such, he argues, that NATO would not be able to use its tactical weapons because there has not been sufficient time for political decisions; moreover the missile sites are likely to have been overrun by then. The Soviets then offer the Germans, Danes, and Norwegians a ceasefire for withdrawal from NATO, neutrality and unlocking of the naval gates to the Atlantic."

Russia's Long-term Aim Succeeding: *Digest Weekly Review,* **Gloucestershire, England.**

"Russia is on the very point of achieving one of its long-term aims, that of establishing a belt of pro-Russian countries stretching from the eastern Mediterranean ports to the Persian Gulf. Should Syria take over Lebanon, and the leftwing activists completely control Iran, then Russia will have an unbroken line of Pro-Soviet States from the Mediterranean to the borders of India, Lebanon, Syria, Iraq, Iran and Afghanistan.

"This has very nearly been achieved, and once established, the Western Powers can say goodbye to Middle East oil and its outlets. . . . Russia already controls the entrance to the Red Sea with Aden, Ethiopia and the Yemen, and aided by Britain and America, the South Africans are to be forced to hand over the vital port of Walvis Bay to left-wing leaders. Although most of this is obvious to any student of international affairs, the appalling naivety of Britain and America's political leaders passes belief." G.J. Keegan, Jr., blamed the CIA, the diplomatic corps, the State Department and educators for attempting the cover-up in naive hopes for peace. He said that after he exhausted every potential to rectify this tragic situation, he had one other alternative and that was to retire and tell it like it is.

"As a result, Keegan added there have been efforts to intimidate and silence him. 'Let me assure you that the price of speaking out comes very high.'

"The world today is under assault by the most active and aggressive imperialism in recorded history from the Kremlin and associated Communist parties all over the world. After 60 years of aggression by the Soviets, only 17% of the remaining world population lives in what could be termed a free society, Keegan emphasized. And he added, the rate of decline is 6% per year. The general, a former assistant chief of staff for Air Force intelligence, concludes that the Soviets are going through the most extensive war preparations in peacetime history. The history of the 1930's, when Adoph Hitler was preparing Nazi Germany for World War, was compared with present times and the U.S. government's failure to recognize the Soviet Union's threat of attack. On the eve of World War Number Two, British Intelligence knew Nazi Germany was fully prepared to go to war, according to a book written by a Winston Churchill aide, the general said."

Soviet Particle-Beam Weapon Update: *UPI, Washington,* **May, 1979.**

"After having dismissed evidence that the Soviet Union is developing particle beam weapons, the Defense Department is exploring the possibility of such 'killer rays.' The beams, fired from satellites parked in space, could destroy enemy ICBMs just after launch.

"In May, 1977, *Aviation Week & Space Technology* magazine published details of Soviet tests of charged particle beam weapons and development plans. 'Our story was greeted with the same high-level official sneering that has been the initial government reaction to every new Soviet weapons development of the past 20 years,' said Robert Hotz, editor and publisher. He said President Carter and Defense Secretary Harold Brown 17 months ago dismissed the weapons as technically impossible.

"Hotz said particle beam weapons offer the promise of reducing strategic nuclear weapons to a negligible factor in the future. . . . If the Soviets achieve this capability first, it will give them enormous, crucial leverage in imposing their political will on the rest of the world. If the U.S. achieves it first, there will be no need for flimsy SALT agreements, and the threat of Soviet nuclear blackmail will lose its credibility.

"The article said eight successful Soviet experiments have been detected propagating electron beams in the ionosphere and in outer space from Cosmos unmanned spacecraft, manned Soyuz transport spacecraft and from the Salyut manned space station.

"Soviet ground-based, charge particle beam propagation tests against targets at Sarova near Gorki also have been detected, it said. The tests are believed to be a prelude to a ground based anti-missile system for 1980."

If the Soviets achieve this, we are all done for! But of course our President and Secretary of Defense, in spite of the mounting evidence for its presence in the Soviet laboratories, says it can't be done!

This same Grade One intelligence was manifested by others in days gone by who said; "Man will never fly to the moon!"

From the foregoing documented statements, (many of them from men who know, for they have been there and/or have been directly involved in watching the Soviet movements firsthand in Europe and in Russia itself), we have a great deal of evidence supporting the fact that we will have THE COMING OIL WAR in the not-too-distant future! From the same remarks it is evident that the United States is presently unprepared. But you can help yourself as an individual family to be prepared both physically and spiritually.

Chapter 5
The Reasons For The War

This oil war would never have taken place in a million years had capitalism not fed Communism for over 50 years.

Communism would never make it economically without capitalistic aid of a constant nature, most of it from the United States.

Unbelievably, the capitalists of Wall Street have actually financed Communism. Without this money-making venture for the capitalists, Communism would have been overthrown by now and the world would not be facing the coming oil war.

The founding fathers of the United States knew what they were doing. They had experienced the tyranny of Europe's systems and wanted a new country free of government powers and banking interests controlling every money-making enterprise.

The Constitution of the United States is the greatest document ever written for the freedoms of man and his pursuit of happiness (outside of the Bible itself).

Basically, it is an expression of the freedoms indicated by the Bible, inasmuch as the Bible supports free enterprise and the right to happiness for all mankind.

Our forefathers of this Republic created a majestic document limiting the government of man over man. It was a limitation of government that they formed, leaving man to his own free will and incentive to create a free-enterprise system for the good of all. And it worked! It has been utterly fantastic and incredible what the system has done in 200 years. Every American should hold his head high and praise God for the men who produced limited government.

The World Leader

As was mentioned earlier in this book, America has produced the most innovative of the world's thinkers, doers, creators, inventors, and discoverers. America has produced the most outstanding array of necessities and luxuries in human history. Europe and Asia and the other parts of the world traveled by horse-and-buggy, horseback, and water buffalo; shipped via waterways on primitive boats or steamship lines fueled by coal, or overland by coal-belching trains (in the last century only); heated and cooked and manufactured by simple fire, steam, etc. Then dawned the United States of America. When that happened the world changed.

Science changed. 80 percent of all the scientists the world has ever known are still alive today because they are of today's generation.

Modern transportation came, and communications developed the sophisticated world of today: computers, television, telephones, jets, laser beams, microwave ovens, nuclear power, and a sophisticated array of modern electronic devices that have changed business, home life, communications, and travel like no other century has ever seen or will see again during the next 100 years.

It is hard to believe, but most of the people in Asia and Africa have never seen a television set! They may have heard of them, but they have never seen one operate.

Most of the people of the world do not use flush toilets! It may be hard to comprehend, but most homes in Asia and Africa do not have running water! Most of them don't live in anything as big as your two-car garage. I've been there—South America, Africa, Asia, India, the islands of the sea. It is like this for the majority of people in these areas, although a few rich people do have these amenities.

Most people in Communist countries, especially Asiatic countries under Communism, have no idea how we live with the things we call "necessities." They would be astounded at our riches—riches that have come to the Western nations because of the Free-Enterprise System—not Communism or state control.

Thank God for the freedom-loving country you were born in, and support its freedoms. Outside of eternal life for believers in the hereafter, this is the greatest gift of God for any human being, along with good health.

The Communist World

What does the rest of the world have?

In many cases, pure Communistic control. This means you own nothing and are considered a worker in a classless society, where if you go to college or do not go to college you are paid as they (the government) see fit, and not according to your education, experience, and qualifications, as you would be in a free-enterprise country.

You are deprived of real durable goods, excellent cuts of meat, and delicious foods that the "free enterprisers" enjoy on their tables, because you cannot afford these items. If by some miracle you could afford them, you could not find them in the stores to buy. They are not there. Only the Soviet elite enjoy these things from special stores.

Many times I have been behind the Iron Curtain. Clothes are simply made—no fine tailoring and no styling, as we would seek.

Foods are atrocious by our standards. This includes the foods you buy in a grocery store, like the famed Gum Store in Moscow, or the foods you buy in a restaurant.

I tried roast duck in our hotel one night in Moscow. It arrived one hour later, and to save my life I could not cut it. I tried to hold it with my fork and finally stabbed it with my knife. I could not even break the skin.

I looked around and decided, who cares. I proceeded to pick up the whole duck and sink my teeth into it as hard as I could. My teeth rebounded like they were plunged into a rubber ball. The duck is still in Russia. I ordered another bowl of soup.

In the big cities of India, Thailand, Vietnam, etc., you can order reasonably good or acceptable food in the American-styled hotels. But don't go out of town. WHEW! The food in those areas is totally nonconsumable for you as a Westerner.

Beggars are everywhere. The more professional families have gouged an eye out of their children or chopped off one of their hands so they can beg more effectively, appealing to the sympathy of the "rich American."

The Sophisticated Communist

Now we come to the more sophisticated Communists for a moment, the ones in Russia and behind the Iron Curtain.

For example, you could go to East Berlin and to West Berlin. The business is booming on the free-enterprise side of the Wall of Berlin. It looks like death warmed over on the East (Communist) side. I know. I've been there driving down Karl Marx Square.

After you have left London or New York, drive through the streets of Moscow for a couple of days. Look at the gray, drab, miserably crowded apartment buildings, where thousands live in squalor and need. I have.

In spite of what the Communists brag they have done, they could not and would not believe, when I told them, how we lived in Canada and the United States. This was only for the super-rich, in their minds.

Cars, telephones, bathtubs—most Russian homes have none. Three-bedroom apartments are unheard-of. Many families live together in squalor.

The toilets in these "modern buildings" are the old-fashioned kind with the water container up near the ceiling. You pull the old cord to release the water to flush the toilet.

As you sit there, looking around, you wonder how long that water container has been up over your head, and what is more pertinent to the moment, will it fall on your head as you pull the rope? I was lucky!

You cannot buy gum in the Gum Store, nor candy as we know it. Their ice cream is like ice milk, and so on.

But how did the Communists get where they are today even by their standards, and how did they reach such a superior position militarily? There is one answer.

The capitalists (greedy capitalists without ethical principles) loaned them great amounts of money at low interest, gave them great benefits, and sold them secrets, scientific knowledge, and American expertise, experience, and abilities. They took it and gladly used it, and built their Communistic empire on American and European capital.

Without this capital aid from the countries which they hated and vowed to destroy, they would be destroyed today themselves.

But greedy international bankers, who hold allegiance to no country, made the deals and financed Communism in order to make money regardless of the international military consequences of the next generation. Many of those corrupt capitalists are still alive today.

The Free-Enterprise System

In the total liberty of no government controls, America grew on the Free-Enterprise System as no society ever has. There were no restraints from making an honest living. Let men produce what other people need or want. The law of Supply and Demand determined creations, productions, inventions, discoveries, quantities, and qualities. It made money for all, for all could engage in competitive production, sales, and exchanges of goods for goods or goods for money.

Day after day, people do business for the good of all. Room is made for virtually every honest man and woman to make it in America. Millions of immigrants who came penniless to this country (including me) have made it! We made it, you made it, because the government stayed out of business deals, and you operated on your own initiative, ambition, honesty, and creative powers. It was and is wonderful.

I entered the United States with 25 dollars in my pocket in 1948. The next 30 years would see this Canadian rise and fall and rise again in business. I came with next to nothing in my pocket on a Greyhound bus, and then hitchhiked all around while going to college. I lived to see the day when year after year I could drive a new car because of the free-enterprise system and God's direct leading in my life.

There are millions of failure-and-success stories in this country. Self-made millionaries abound. FREE ENTERPRISE gave us the opportunities. We thank God for it.

I had the opportunity of turning my million-dollar book sales into my personal ministry. I never needed a million dollars and still don't. I felt that if God gave this opportunity to me in this great country, I should take a comfortable living from it for my family and turn back what money I could into helping others find the happiness spiritually and economically I had found in Christian America. What a country! What a God!

The free market in America asks and answers a million questions every hour, if not every minute. Decisions for business are made every second we live here—decisions that will generate a simple living for the man on the street in business for himself, or decisions that will affect the lives of millions of people and bring in billions of dollars. The free market moves on daily.

We do not have to fill out papers for a government bureaucracy for them to finally, months later, tell us whether we can plant, build, do, go, produce, excavate, manufacture, etc., etc., as they do in Communist countries. They don't even ask over there anymore. They just look for a job through the hierarchy's offices of employment and take what they are told to accept—at any wages, hours, and physical labor. They have no choice, no freedoms, no opportunities to speak their mind. They fill out forms, wait endless hours, have appointments with government agencies, and eke out a living for their family that you would actually cry over, if you really understood your Soviet counterpart in daily human life.

The Principles of Freedom

Individual liberty is the chief characteristic of our system. Complete control is the chief characteristic of Communism.

Productivity is the result of our system. Lack of economic productivity and agricultural development is the most obvious result of their enigmatic system.

Self-reliance is the key personal principle here. Government reliance is the key there. Here we have plenty of whatever we need. There they have a million unsatisfied needs, wants, empty store shelves, and empty streets. Their government purchases from the Western free-enterprise nations the things they cannot and do not produce, have never produced and do not have the ability to produce.

It takes capital to produce a booming, productive economy—capital generated in a free-market exchange of goods and services, where men can use their talents and brains to make contracts and work for the betterment of their society without government restraints.

The Communists have to borrow from the governments and corporations who enjoy this type of freedom—in other words, from the free-enterprise system.

Without billions of dollars borrowed from the capitalists in loans, goods, machinery, and services, the Communists wouldn't be anywhere today. The Judeo-Christian principle of free enterprise (found in countries following the

Judeo-Christian principle of freedom for all) sponsors growth, contentment, competition, development, production, and the greatest degree of happiness known to mankind on earth.

A classic example of feudalism and poverty was Japan prior to 1945. In the years following 1945, the introduction of the free-enterprise system, accompanied by the scientific expertise of America, has made this tiny country the "U.S.A. of the Oriental world." Fifty years ago Japan was an extremely poor, illiterate nation of people going nowhere. Look at her today. Free enterprise works.

Our Mistake

But because some of these capitalists got greedy and avaricious in their nature, Communism thrived when it would have died.

And the same terrible mistake we made with Russia, we are now making with China where the average person makes 19 to 25 cents a day.

Where would China be today without the Western nations' capitalistic aid, science, expertise, and services? She would accomplish virtually nothing.

We aided Russia, and in turn Russia aided China for the past 30 years, or there would be much less than what you see now in "modern" China.

Pick up one of the new books flooding the market today about "modern China." There is nothing modern by our standards. Most of the people have never seen a flush toilet or TV, and only by the skin of their teeth (or a government handout) do they have a transistor radio, and then only because the government wanted to communicate more readily with the population.

But compare thriving, booming, bursting Hong Kong, just over the border. There the Chinese had and have the free-enterprise system of the British Empire. Even the Communists use this free system for the open marketing of their Communist-made goods!

Possibly Hong Kong and Berlin give the most dramatic differences seen by the naked eye today.

Sometimes it is unbelievable. But it is real.

William E. Simon, former U.S. Secretary of the Treasury, says in his excellent book, *A Time for Truth,* that the free-enterprise system has worked so well that—

96 percent of all U.S. homes have a telephone.

50 percent of all Americans own one or more cars.

96 percent of all American homes have at least one television set.

After American farmers finish feeding the U.S. population, they export 60 percent of their wheat and rice, 50 percent of their soybeans, one-quarter of their grain sorghum, and one-fifth of their corn. The U.S. provides half of the world's wheat.

American farms produce this despite the fact that since 1940 the number of U.S. farms and farm workers has decreased by two-thirds. During that time, however, agricultural productivity has increased by 75 percent!

The Contrasts

All of this comes from a complete lack of government control. We are free from government powers, we are left to the individual free-enterprise system.

In Communism, freedom of the individual is destroyed.

In our system, it is pursued for the good of all.

In Communism, the state takes over all property.

In our system, you can buy anything for sale if you have the money.

In Communism, you are told what to work at and what your salary will be.

In our system, you educate yourself to be what you want when you wish, and you determine your own salary by negotiating on education or experience. The sky is the limit.

Their system destroys initiative.

Ours enhances it, initiates it, and enjoys it.

Their system supposedly "liberates people" by enslav - ing them to the demands of the state.

Communists throw men and women into horrible prisons and and slave farms in the frozen Siberian wasteland for dissenting from the government.

In this country you have complete freedom to buy paper and ink and press, and print virtually what you like.

The Communists throw intellectuals disagreeing with them into psychiatric hospitals and almost throw away the key.

Here you can form a party if you wish and run for the Presidency.

Communists take what wealth they can garner and use it for military conquests the world over. They have to borrow to feed their people with a meager diet.

Here we feed first, and then build a limited war machine for our protective purposes.

There it is deprivation of privilege and personal purpose as you are subjected to the state's directives.

Here you are free to pursue personal purposes (within the law) and are not subjected to state harassment.

The Soviet system just does not work for the people or for the government. Even if it worked for the government, you might say something good about it, but it doesn't. They too have to borrow, beg, steal, cut throats, and depend on American and European capitalism, expertise, and ideas.

After the Revolution that destroyed the czarist economy of Russia, the Communists themselves were faced with revolution, for the promises of the new system were not working and the government was faced with bankruptcy of the system.

It got so bad that they had to abandon pure Communism and embark on a journey of "coexistence with the West" just to exist as a government.

Where the Communists Got Their Money

Lenin stated that the capitalists would do business with anyone, and when Russia was through with them, the Communists would take over the world. The capitalists would sell to them on credit everything they needed to satisfy the needs of the people and to enable the government to secure all economic and military necessities for the takeover of the world. "Industrial cohabitation with the capitalists" was Lenin's phrase, indicating that they could and would compromise the pure doctrine of Communism and commit economic and industrial adultery with their avowed enemies.

And so the industrialization of Russia began. People began to eat sufficiently. Dissenters were squashed, and capital flowed by the billions from the Wall Street bankers and London bankers in return for "profits from Communism."

American and European industrialists fell over their own feet in their zeal to sell to the Soviets. The International Barnsdale Corporation and Standard Oil, for example, won oil-drilling rights; Stuart, James and Cook, Inc., reorganized Russian coal mines. The International General Electric Company sold Moscow electrical equipment. And other major American firms, Westinghouse Du Pont, and RCA, assisted in various ways.

In the thirties our businessmen shipped and installed replicas of complex American production centers to the Soviet Union, where they were assembled like gigantic do-it-yourself kits. The Cleveland firm of Arthur G. Mackee provided the equipment for huge steel plants at Magnitogorsk; John K. Clader of Detroit equipped and installed the material for tractor plants at Chelyabinsk; Henry Ford and the Austin Company provided all the elements for a major automobile works at Gorki. Colonel Hugh Cooper, creator of the Mussel Shoals Dam, planned and built the giant hydroelectric installation at Dniepostroi.

The most grandiose Bolshevik achievements of the thirties, which glorified Communism throughout the world and convinced two generations of American and European intellectuals of the economic potency of the USSR and of centralized planning, were all achievements of Western capitalism!

By 1941 the Soviet Union was desperately begging the West for aid against Hitler's armies. The phenomenon known as lend-lease was created. Between 1941 and 1945 a vast flood of goods was flown and shipped to Russia: raw materials, machinery, tools, complete industrial plants, spare parts, textiles, clothing, canned meat, sugar, flour, fats, and purely military supplies—an unending stream of weapons, trucks, tanks, aircraft, and gasoline. Lend-lease was equal to more than a third of prewar level of Soviet production—a gift of at least 11 billion dollars worth of the most advanced technology in the world!

Shockingly, many wealthy American families jumped on the Soviet bandwagon and loaned money, knowing full well that the bloody revolution caused millions of deaths in Russia.

Not long after the Bolshevik Revolution, the Rockefeller-owned Standard Oil of New Jersey bought half of the huge Caucasus oil fields. In 1927, Standard Oil of New York built a large refinery in Russia, helping to put the Russians back on their feet.

Shortly after that, Standard Oil of New York and its subsidiary, Vacuum Oil Company, concluded a deal to market Soviet oil in European countries, and it was reported that a loan of 75 million dollars to the Bolsheviks was arranged.

Wherever Standard Oil would go, Chase National Bank was sure to follow. (The Rockefellers' Chase Bank was later merged with the Warburg's Manhattan Bank to form the Chase Manhattan Bank.)

Chase National Bank and the Equitable Trust Company were originally leaders in the Soviet credit business.

The Rockefellers' Chase National Bank was also involved in selling Bolshevik bonds in the U.S. in 1928. Patriotic organizations denounced the Chase for doing so.

Congressmen Louis McFadden, chairman of the House Banking Committee, maintained in a speech to his fellow Congressmen:

> *The Soviet government has been given United States Treasury funds by the Federal Reserve Banks and Board through the Chase Bank and Guarantee Trust Company and other banks in New York.*
>
> *Open up the books of the Amtorg, the trading organization of the Soviet government in New York, and of Gostorg, the general office of the Soviet Trade Organization, and of the State Bank of the Union of Soviet Socialist Republics, and you will be staggered to see how much American money has been taken from the United States Treasury for the benefit of Russia. Find out what business has been transacted for the State Bank of Soviet Russia by its correspondent, the Chase Bank of New York (Congressional Record, June 15, 1933).*

Our Energy Mess

IF WE HAD NOT FINANCED THE COMMUNISTS ORIGINALLY, AND KEEP ON FINANCING THEM, WE WOULD NOT HAVE TO FIGHT THEM IN THE COMING OIL WAR.

The second reason we are going to have to fight the oil war is our utter dependence on foreign oil, and our undeveloped domestic energy sources.

Government regulations on the private energy industries of the U.S., capable of producing all the energy this country could ever use, are stifling, crippling, and suppressing development of these immensely needed products, and are making us totally dependent on the Arabs for what we could be producing ourselves.

When the government of this country lets the free-enterprise system work, the businesses large and small will run themselves on a purely market-need basis. The public will receive what it needs and is prepared to pay for. Wages and prices will once again stabilize. The government will have a much lower budget, for it won't be subsidizing industries to keep them alive.

U.S. energy production is down, but demands are up from every sector of the country. We are not self sufficient, *but we could be*. We depend on foreign energy now for over 48 percent of our energy needs.

According to U.S. government statistics we have the following situation:

We have enough coal to last 800 years at today's rate of consumption. Over half of all the coal reserves in the free world are here in the U.S.

Natural gas is in plenteous supply now, with over 920 trillion cubic feet in reserves.

We have from 50 to 127 billion barrels of oil still untapped in America. There are also well over 40 billion barrels in the Outer Continental Shelf. (We have only explored about 5 percent of it.)

Nuclear power, properly and safely developed, could supply a great percentage of the energy needs of this country for uncounted centuries. There are many areas yet unexplored where clean, efficient, nuclear power could do the job in industrial, business, and home-related realms.

Regulations of the government sponsored by environmentalists, Communists, and lobbyists from other energy sources, have strangled our development and made us dependent on foreign oil.

By dropping price controls, deregulating the energy industries, stopping expensive subsidies, and getting rid of government-imposed destructive bans, the general marketplace would settle down very shortly in pricing for oil, gas, and all kinds of energy needs.

The market would run itself, and demand would determine exploration. The motive of "profit for effort" would create greater and greater exploration and development right here on home soil. We would never need foreign oil-energy again.

Keep in mind that Senator Edward Kennedy helped produce the Energy Conservation and Production Act, and that President Carter has swung right in with it. This Act stifles production, exploration, our businesses, homes, and industries.

We now have a giant bureaucracy set up by the President to control all aspects of energy needs, pricing, etc., centralizing control of energy in Washington, stifling development, taking it out of the hands of the general marketplace, and giving us a government dictatorship, which will eventually force us to go to war for a foreign energy.

We should demand that our government give back to us the free-enterprise system in the energy industries. Then watch production and pricing be properly set within 6 to 12 months.

Control of the oil industry is done by the "seven sisters" right here in the mainland of the United States. We will now address ourselves to them and their phenomenal power in Washington and in OPEC. The "seven sisters" are Exxon, Mobil, Standard, Socal, Shell, Texaco, and Arco. It is now time to look at who controls oil, where it is, and what will happen shortly.

Chapter 6
The Mighty Shadow Government

Government in the shadows is a subject for a book by itself, and many people attempted to tell the sinister story of the BANKING AND OIL MOGULS, who, through their multinational corporations and vast powerful political machinery, have manipulated entire countries into the palms of their hands.

They are doing this more than ever today. Facts will substantiate that fact right here in America. And in the OPEC (Oil Producing Exporting Nations) cartel, great influence is brought to bear by the oil companies who drilled the wells in the beginning and by the bankers who loaned the money in the beginning for the purpose of continued exploration and development of the oil industries.

There is a professionally estimated 2000 billion barrels of oil in the world today. Fifteen percent had been used through 1973 (297 billion barrels). Thirty-seven percent, or 740 billion barrels, are in the form of proved and prospective reserves, and about 48 percent, or 963 billion barrels, are in the form of undiscovered potential, according to J. D. Moody of Mobil Oil, at the Ninth World Petroleum Congress in Tokyo in May of 1975.

Where is all this oil?

Outside Russia, most of the known oil reserves are in the Middle Eastern countries of Saudi Arabia, Iraq, Iran, Kuwait, Bahrein, Abu Dhabi, and Qatan. Large reserves are also in Venezuela, Libya, Nigeria, Algeria, and Indonesia, plus Mexico, Canada, and the United States, along with a little in the North Sea next to Britain.

Prior to the sixties, most oil was being produced in North America. But the picture soon changed as we set up more regulations by government over mining procedures and refinement, and in other ways. This was part of the mistake that we are suffering for today.

The Seven Sisters

Now we have the "seven international sisters" producing 91 percent of the Middle East's crude oil and 77 percent of the free world's supply outside the United States, in addition to what they produce here.

The British and the Dutch controlled much of the Middle East oil exploration and development until the middle of the twenties, when the "seven sisters" started through negotiations with the British, Dutch, and oil countries to buy into powerful positions with American banking money, *which they also controlled to a large extent.* The oil companies were, and are even more today, tied into the big commercial banking interests of the United States through ownerships, partnerships, and agreements, and through mutual directorships in dozens of instances.

To say that the international bankers control the oil men, or that the oil barons control the bankers, is to miss the point. They are virtually one and the same. *The same men own and control both.* They run the banks and run the oil industry, from exploration for crude oil to the final operation of putting it into your tank as you drive up.

The banks did come first, however, in the scenario of the "chicken and the egg." However, in more than one instance it was vast amounts of oil money that produced great banking institutions in America.

After much painstaking effort, the Americans got into the Middle East and almost wiped out the British and the Dutch in securing control over all drilling, exploration, and extracting of crude oil from the area. They now control vast amounts of areas, to the exclusion of other countries and the independents, who would still like to get in (and periodically do pop up here and there).

They are either bought out or forced out by the "seven

sisters," who act as an oil cartel in themselves. The fact that they are a cartel is evidenced by the fact that others cannot buy into the industry in the countries where the oil lies.

The "seven sisters" have done their best to squeeze the independent oil companies out of business in North America. When you control most REFINEMENT, in YOUR OWN refineries, you do not have to sell much to the independents. They are then squeezed out of business.

Black Ink and Red Faces

This report is from the Honolulu *Star-Bulletin,* Thursday, October 25, 1979.

NEW YORK (AP) — Reports of big profits by the big oil companies, which have outraged some members of Congress, are coming as a surprise to the experts who keep an eye on the industry for investors.

"The big surge in third-quarter earnings is causing an embarrassment to the oil companies and the oil analytical fraternity," said one member of that fraternity, Sanford Margoshes of Shearson Hayden Stone.

He and other analysts had predicted sizable increases in the companies' profits in the third quarter over the comparable 1978 quarter, generally between 40 percent and 60 percent, but only a handful have been in that range. Most have been much more spectacular.

Phillips Petroleum Co., the nation's 11th-largest oil company, today reported a 62 percent increase in profits for the quarter, an increase it attributed primarily to increased chemical earnings and to profits from overseas oil operations.

Ashland Oil, ranked 15th in the industry, bucked the trend today and reported a 14.5 percent decline in operation earnings for the latest quarter. The company attributed the downturn largely to reduced earnings from its coal and construction operations.

Standard Oil Co. (Ohio), the 14th-biggest U.S. Oil company, announced the biggest profit increase for July-to-September period: a 191 percent jump.

Mobil Corp., the nation's second-largest oil company, weighed in late in the day with a 131 percent increase, and 10th-ranked Sun Co. said its profits rose 65 percent in the quarter. Cities Service Co. and Marathon Oil Co., both ranked about 17th among U.S. oil companies, reported profits up 64 percent and 58 percent, respectively.

The announcement of those dramatic profit increases followed a 118 percent jump announced Monday by Exxon Corp., the industry giant, and a 134 percent increase announced Tuesday by Conoco.

Mobile, attributing its profits increase to better results from foreign operations, said its earnings for the quarter were $595 million, or $2.80 a share, compared with $252 million, or $1.22 a share, 12 months earlier. Sales rose from $9.2 billion to $12.1 billion.

Sohio said its profits rose from $125.7 million, or $1.06 a share, to $366.2 million, or $3.03 a share. Higher prices for Alaskan oil were the main reasons for the earnings increase, Sohio said. The firm said sales rose in the quarter from $1.3 billion to $2.1 billion.

Sun said its quarterly profits were $174.3 million, or $3.19 a share, up from $105.4 million, or $1.97 a share, in the 1978 period. Sales rose to $2.61 billion from $1.83 billion. Sun attributed the improved quarterly and year-to-date results to higher profits overseas and in the company's Canadian unit, Suncor.

Cities Service said its quarterly profits rose from $52.6 million, or $1.91 a share, in the 1978 period, to $86.1 million, or $3.11 a share. The company ascribed the increase to higher domestic oil, gas, and copper prices. Sales rose from $1.14 billion to $1.6 billion.

Marathon said third-quarter profits rose from $50.5 million, or 83 cents a share, in the third quarter last year, to $79.7 million, or $1.31 a share, mostly due to better results from foreign operations. Sales for Marathon were

$1.91 billion in the third quarter, up from $1.2 billion in the year-earlier quarter.

Phillips said its profits for the quarter rose to $193.0 million, or $1.25 a share, from $118.8 million or 77 cents a share in the same quarter last year. Revenues rose from $1.75 billion to $2.50 billion.

The Seven Sisters and the Banks

Who owns the "seven sisters"? Who has their stock? With what banks do they share directorships and exchanges of great power? In a study done by the Securities and Exchange Commission, it is reported that for the Exxon, Mobil, and Socal companies, the combined holdings of the Rockefeller families and family foundations carry an amount of influence equal to working control in all three.

In a further examination of the intriguing subject of Rockefeller-controlled oil companies and banks, you will find that Exxon, Mobil, Standard of Indiana, and Socal-Standard of California own 32 percent of domestic reserves of oil and over 30 percent of domestic refining capacity, and that they make over 26 percent of all retail sales in America. The Rockefellers hold controlling interest in these companies (to say nothing of other major and minor companies), and have interlocking directorates: directors of Exxon and Standard Oil come together as directors of Chase Manhattan Bank, and directors of Exxon and Mobil are directors on the Chemical Bank of New York. This is the biggest business arrangement I know of!

In an enlarged survey you will find that the interlocking directorates are as follows:

Exxon is tied in with Chase Manhattan, Morgan Guarantee, and Chemical Bank.

Mobil is interconnected with First National City, Bankers Trust, and Chemical Bank.

Standard of Indiana is tied in with Chase Manhattan, Continental Illinois, and National Bank and Trust.

Socal is connected to Bank of America and Western Bancorporation.

Shell is connected with First National City Bank.

Texaco is tied in with Chemical Bank and Continental.

These banks have interlocking directors in oil companies. Directors of one bank are directors in another bank, and so on. The connection is so obvious.

Antitrust suits have failed to destroy the interlocking powers that control so much of the nation in many hidden corporations whose interlocking directorships are well-hidden by committees, boards, and directors all down the long line. It was and is difficult to see who controls who and what—who is the final benefactor in all of these. But obviously powerful business associates are connected.

Powerful lobbyists from the banking and oil industries have kept the truth hidden. Money talks.

So far in the past decade of the seventies it appears that with the exception of Gulf and SoCal, all eight of the largest oil companies are interlocked through large commercial banks with at least one other member of the top group of companies. Exxon is tied in with three others—Mobil, Standard, and Texaco. Mobil is also tied in with three—Exxon, Shell, and Texaco. And so on it goes with interlocking directorates and controls. Acting as their own cartel, they control the industry, freezing others out.

It is known that whenever six of the country's major commercial banks get together to hold their board meetings, the directors of the top eight oil companies (except Gulf and SoCal) meet with directors of their largest corporations.

When the famed and very large Bank of America conducts its board meetings, directors of SoCal, Union, and Getty oil companies sit down together with them. Shell and Mobil meet with the directors of First National City Bank.

More Control

In addition to intercorporate relationships with one

another, the oil companies with their interlocking directorates have unified control and ownership of the oil pipelines domestically and abroad.

By controlling these arteries, they can restrict the flow of crude oil to the independent dealers in many ways. They can act as a cartel in limiting supplies to the refineries and can thus limit supplies of gas to gas stations and the consuming public, which lately has been the case.

There is no shortage of crude oil in storage in the country now. But there has been a shortage of refining, and thus a shortage for the consumer, and thus long lines for filling up.

Every important pipeline in the world is controlled by the "seven sisters."

There is the 753-mile pipeline known as the Trans-Arabian Pipeline from Qaisuma, Saudi Arabia, to the Mediterranean Sea. It is owned by Exxon, SoCal, Texaco, and Mobil. Exxon alone owns the 1100-mile Interprovincial Pipeline in Canada, and also the 143-mile pipeline in Venezuela. This is to say nothing of the lines in Iraq, Iran, and neighboring areas of the Middle East.

They have the offshore leases under joint ownership also. Much of this is federal land. Somewhere down the line, the federal government sold and granted leases to consortiums of the oil industry—the "seven sisters"—to the exclusion of many of the minor competing companies. It is a well-known fact that many senators and members of the House of Representatives have stock in the "seven sisters" cartel. It would not be hard to imagine how the sales went in this direction.

If you know that your stock and stock options would rise phenomenally by a certain vote for a certain company or group of companies to get the offshore leases, it would appear financially advantageous to make sure they got the land.

Now take all this foreign oil, oil shipping, pipeline control, and refining process, and place it in the bankers' hands. Add to that the domestic oil of America and its refining, shipping, and processing to final products, and place *that* in the bankers' hands!

The Bankers' Schemes

Some of these banks that are now multinational have set up their subsidiary banking agencies all over the world (not subject to U.S. banking regulatory restrictions), and especially in the Soviet Union, aiding the Soviets in every way to accomplish their desired military goals and general overall industrial achievements.

In the history of every war it was the international banks and bankers that came out on top by lending money to both sides—money with which to provide armaments for the war and to generally finance the entire conflict.

Economic and banking history is full of how this happened time and time again in Europe and even in the Civil War of the U.S. It was banking money from England and France from the House of Rothschild's banks that financed the war between the north and the south in the U.S. in the last century.

International banking money financed the Bolshevik Revolution, and international banking money is financing the rise of Communism in Russia and China today. Is this justifiable capitalism?

Some of the main lobbyists and deeply interested parties in present negotiations leading to the final recognition of mainland China by the United States were and are the international bankers.

They will loan China the money to buy American products. They will also sell China the products through their subsidiary corporations that manufacture what China needs, from computer science to rubber tires.

The bankers who control the oil and then branch out into a thousand business directions hold in their hand the power to definitely control and guide government decisions.

Add a final and guiding factor. The Rockefeller-controlled Council on Foreign Relations in New York City supplies most of the major leaders of this country to the White House Staff.

Either through the Council on Foreign Relations or their new organization, the Trilateral Commission, we receive most of the appointed staff members of the President's Cabinet today. These organizations want to control the foregoing policy-making of the United States government. They also, of course, virtually succeeded in doing so. Almost every Secretary of State, Secretary of Defense, Secretary of the Treasury, National Security Advisor, etc., has come from the CFR. Over 75 percent of the men next to our President today have come through this "school."

We have the following men occupying powerful positions that have come through the CFR or the Trilateral Commission:

Jimmy Carter, Walter Mondale, Zbigniew Brzezinski , Michael Blumenthal, Harold Brown, Cyrus Vance, etc., etc.

For a more complete rundown on who runs the country and where they came from, read my survival book entitled HOW TO SURVIVE THE MONEY CRASH, which explores banking and other areas of the monetary systems of the world.

The international bankers control the Council on Foreign Relations and the Trilateral Commission. They set up these organizations in their beginnings.

Now they control the oil, the money flow, the political flow of politicians here and abroad in many instances, and through the tremendous power that great amounts of money can generate, they partially control entire countries and the future of the world!

They can and have in the past encouraged wars and discouraged wars. They finance them and sit back getting richer and richer as warring nations borrow billions and pay interest on this money through taxation to fight their wars. The people of the country eventually finance the wars by paying back through increased taxation by the government.

World Control

Like a giant mosaic, the pattern of power emerges as you go further up the line. When you place the pieces of the puzzle together you finally get the entire message: THE WORLD IS CONTROLLED BY THE BANKING-OIL BARONS, AND THEY HAVE THE POWER IN THEIR HANDS TO CONTROL THE DESTINIES OF NA-TIONS AND THUS THE DESTINIES OF BILLIONS OF PEOPLE.

Antony Sutton states in the *Trilateral Observer* that the basic Trilateral Commission structure is a power pyramid. At the tip of the pyramid we can identify a "financial mafia," comprising several old-line American families, the American aristocracy. Below this highest level is the Executive Committee for the U.S., linked to members of Executive Committees in Europe and Japan. Next comes the Trilateral Commission itself: 109 members from North America, 106 from Europe, and 74 from Japan (all of whom are the top- bankers-industrialists and politicans of the areas).

Trilaterals control the executive branch of our government here, and so control their policies. An ongoing project is to dominate nine core countries in Europe and Japan and by virtue of their productivity account for 80 percent of the world output! The "core" group can then easily dominate the remaining 20 percent of the world.

The American multinationals provide country-by-country liaison, intelligence, and conduits—the sinews to bind a global new world order to the directions of the financial mafia.

Sutton says that the Trilaterals have rejected the U.S. Constitution and the democratic political process, and that their objective is to obtain the wealth of the world for their own use under the pretense of "public service."

Another one of their ultimate goals is one-world government, with them in complete control. This is their chief control, for the raping of the world's money. They are rapidly achieving it.

Where they are being fought in the world—i.e., by some leaders in the United States, Canada, Europe—they will render these men useless and powerless through wars and planned depressions.

If a nation like the United States is too powerful to be totally controlled by them, they can plan a depression or a major war, and through loans and giant manipulations of money, men, and politics they will finally win the complete control they desire. *It will mean a dictatorship for the United States of America in a totally socialistic government controlled by the international bankers.*

Inasmuch as the international bankers are the owners and leaders of the commercial banks of the world, including the Federal Reserve System in the United States, they can control depressions, recessions, and prosperity.

They largely control this country. The U.S. government is involved to a limited extent in the Federal Reserve Banking System, but only limitedly. *There is a giant shadow government!*

The Federal Reserve

The Federal Reserve System is not "federal" at all. It is completely privately owned and almost privately run. The government has a Federal Reserve Board, but that board only acts as liaison between the System and Government-correlating policies.

The Federal Reserve is privately controlled by the international bankers, who are in control of other banks, commercial banks, oil corporations, and many other kinds of corporations. It is almost impossible to trace final ownership of commercial banks, oil corporations, and many other kinds of corporations. It is almost impossible to trace final ownership of some major stock shares of the largest corporations in the U.S. and the world. Their shares are hidden in corporate names, individual names, foreign names, attorney names, etc.

But it is known that the Federal Reserve is not owned by the government. The FED prints the money needed by the government for the government. The government then pays the FED bonds for the bills printed by the FED. The bonds are paid off with high interest to the FED by the government (with the taxpayers' money, of course).

Presently we have a 532-billion-dollar budget for the federal government—the highest by far for any nation in human history. This is ridiculous. It is absurd. It is inhuman to impose this burden on the American people through taxation.

But the FEDs love it. They print the money and issue the credits for the government. They get the government bonds and interest on the bonds for the money they create to finance (monetize) the federal debt. They love it. They are getting richer and richer as the country gets further and further into debt.

They in turn can sell to the government (through their subsidiary organizations) what the government wants to buy. Again it is money-making for the international bankers.

Don't ask me why our legislators turned the responsibility of printing money over to the international bankers here. I covered that in HOW TO SURVIVE THE MONEY CRASH. It is a terrible situation. We should nationalize the FED immediately, but we won't. It has gone too far now. It is too late to turn back. Only one powerful president and congress could do it. I do not see that in the political future of this country at all, unfortunately.

The FED through the Open Market Committee (that meets every three weeks in Washington) determines interest rates for the banks and the consumers of the nation.

They also determine what happens to the economy of the nation through these interest rates that the Federal Reserve Banks charge the domestic banks for money. The rate is passed on down the line to the businesses and individuals who want the money in loans and credits. If the interest rate is high, the economy is slowed down terribly. Business is then curtailed.

If the rates are low, we have money in circulation, business is booming, and the economy of the country is high.

The FED determines the money supply for the nation—that is, how much money is actually printed and in circulation for the nation. They also determine how much credit money is available. As you know, not all transactions are carried on in dollar bills. Most transactions are on paper, representing credit or dollars on deposit by corporations.

The FED determines the total money supply for the country. Too much money supply can undermine the value of the dollars they print, as we have now. Inflation is simply printing too much money for the nation; the dollar value then goes down, and the prices of products rise.

Too much money being issued by the FED along with restrictive interest rates at the same time, means an injured economy. The government, is using most of the FED money as it is issued. The nation is getting a tight money supply, and thus business is down. Businesses sell less, produce less, manufacture less, and lay off more employees, exactly as is happening now in the United States and Canada, as well as in other countries.

The owners of the FED know exactly what they are doing. They are reducing the powers of the United States domestically through their monetary policies of money issuance and interest rates. They are reducing the power of the U.S. by hiking the cost of gas and oil through contrived shortages. They are reducing the mighty free-enterprise system to ashes by their control of banking, oil, subsidiary corporations, and the Federal Reserve System for the country.

While they are reducing the riches here, and reducing the power of the government, they are enriching Russia and China. Are they trying to bring about a parity of the giant nations? Are they succeeding in reducing the U.S. and increasing the Soviets? And now are they working for China too, thus producing an equality of powers among the big nations and areas, making it harder and harder for one power to be above another? As a consequence of this, will it be much easier to produce the one-world government soon?

The international bankers not only control the FED, but they further create inflation in this country, crippling the nation eventually by the fractional reserve system ratified by the Congress.

Would you believe that the big banks create money out of nothing? Credit-card creation is highly inflationary as it creates money from nothing for users and issuers. Banks created this.

The Fractional Reserve System is a system in which the banks, upon receiving your $1000 deposit in your savings account, can create on paper $7000 more dollars *that do not exist at all*. But they can say they exist for all intents and purposes, and loan that money (on paper only) out to borrowers at a great rate of interest.

They are making interest on money that does not exist! That is inflationary to the superlative degree.

I understand that in Canada it is much worse than in the U.S. They have a 22-1 ratio, as opposed to our 7-1 ratio.

By creating inflation, the international bankers again have terrific leverage by which to cripple a country through its currency.

The Real Shadows

So there you have it, piece by piece. The shadow government exists. It is internationally powerful and has worked itself into many countries of the Western world, from Australia to England, from France to the North American continent.

The bankers control the banks, the money supply, and the interest rates, and thus they control creation of prosperity and depression. They control oil, and largely its consequent products, prices, and peoples, even to agriculture and industry.

They affect governments and policies by controlling what governments need—money and energy.

They are growing in power every month. From the Council on Foreign Relations in the U.S. they developed the Bilderbergers in Europe and finally the Trilateral Commission in order to involve all three areas of the world's technological development and know-how—the Orient, Europe, and North America. Where do they go from here?

That is one exciting question, and the answer is right on the horizon. Let me show you.

The international bankers will stop at nothing until they gain complete world control. They are close now.

They cannot control all emotions of human beings, however, and when they cannot control them they simply use them as best as possible to further their own avaricious aims at world domination.

They did not create Israel as a nation. They did not create the genocide of the Jew under Hitler. They have not created the Palestinian situation of several million homeless refugees. *But they are using this* to further their world designs.

Keep in mind that the bankers want the world in their hands, and soon. They do not care about national boundary lines and national differences, or locations of races and peoples and of government concerns locally.

They want a type of socialistic dictatorship where capitalism continues, for there is where the money is and the goods are. They want a degree of free enterprise, and would never do what the idiotic Communists have done in confiscating all property, businesses, etc. They want high taxation, as in Sweden and Israel, and will have unbelievable power and wealth through this autocratic socialistic system. They are getting close to their goals and could well achieve them within the decade of the eighties, which is upon us now.

Simultaneously producing inflation and major monetary problems in all Western nations, the bankers are creating the death of fiat money (government-issued paper money in each nation) while causing a tremendous rise in the price and value of gold and silver.

They have tremendous gold and silver holdings. They are growing in economic-financial strength every time a South African Krugerrand rises in price, along with the rising price of silver and platinum.

While the bankers grow unbelievably rich, nations are growing unbelievably poorer, including the North American nations, in spite of their tremendous powers. Our economy is a controlled economy.

Simultaneous with the rise of gold and silver and the demise of domestic currencies through inflating of the species internationally, these international bankers are fomenting war in the Middle East through their OPEC allies, who really want Jerusalem back and the Palestinians on the West Bank.

No National Loyalties

Anti-Semites have said that this is a Jewish conspiracy to control the world. But I see just as many, if not more, Gentiles in this vicious hierarchy. It is a group of families that hold no national allegiance precious to themselves and are totally abandoned to greed, power, money, and world dominance. They see themselves as members of the international set; they are citizens of this world—not nations. They will have their one-world government and will control nations. They will be above nations in the end and will only use them for their own aggrandizement.

By instigating another war in the Middle East, the international bankers profit by the loans to finance it, to all sides involved in it, and by the interest that will be paid for those loans by the governments via the people's taxes.

They profit by selling the articles of war through their subsidiary companies around the world, from munition plants to trucks and tires and foodstuffs. It is an unending vicious circle of control, all pouring billions into the coffers of the elite controlling bankers.

By being in such prominent positions with the Arabs via the oil production and marketing, they have the listening ears of the vast Arab world of power, gold, and politics.

They will exploit the Israelis to their own advantage, even if some of them are Jews themselves. This has been done before, in every race. Look at Africans butchering Africans, Americans who murdered Americans in the Civil War, etc., etc.

It is to the financial advantage of the international bankers to plunge us into war, capitalizing on the fears and frustrations of a bloc of Arabs who are homeless and who are fighting a futile war of attrition against the Israelis.

It is to the political advantage of the international bankers to foment war in the Middle East, involving Russia, the United States, and Europe, along with the Arabs and Israelis.

The war will level America, possibly bring control over the Soviets (in their thinking), bring Europe to its economic knees, and carry the whole Western world to the brink of disaster economically and politically. The world would be ready for their new world order after this horrendous war. The bankers will decide where the battles are fought physically, and they will be long gone from there when the fighting starts. While they and theirs are tucked away in safe harbors of rest and peace, the world will blow itself to smithereens!

Every phase of the world government has been planned

and is set up, ready for implementation in the aftermath of this chaos.

The shadow government is ready to come out of the shadows and show its strength, power, and readiness to "help all unfortunate peoples of the world" who will go to war "against the better judgment" of these "benefactors."

Through "detente" the international bankers have made billions, have helped equalize Russia with America, and have produced a situation that looks like mutual annihilation with no win for either side.

By encouraging SALT I and SALT II they have reduced the capabilities of the U.S. and increased the lagging capabilities of the USSR. Mutual Assured Destruction (MAD) seems inevitable.

The owners of the "seven sisters" will ultimately own the very countries from which they now get oil, with all rights, concessions, grants, nationalization, and joint ownerships ended.

They will have it as their own. Sales to the world will be completely determined by them after this oil war.

Even North Sea exploration and oil reserves could be theirs, along with Soviet oil reserves after the war.

The new world order will be set up in Europe, and if necessary they won't mind moving world headquarters to Jerusalem or somewhere in the Middle East. Has it not been said that Israel is the bridge to three continents?

Not all bankers understand what is going on in the system. Only a comparative handful of families are involved. The local banking establishment in your town probably knows nothing of what I have written in this book. The hierarchy is in Europe and New York. Even employees in the banks and oil companies involved know nothing of what is going on. So don't aim your psychological gun at the local employees. They live much like you do.

International Banking

It is not easy to trace, but I have learned that international banking was originally set up by the House of Rothschild. We can thank Meyer Amchel Rothschild, founder of the Bank of England, France, and Germany, for across-the-border international banking. He placed his son Carl over the Bank of Naples, James over the Bank of France, Edmund over the Bank of Germany, Solomon over the Bank of Vienna, and Nathan over the Bank of England.

From this tiny beginning the international bankers took hold, and then burst forth with greed and avarice to control the politics of the world to their own aggrandizement. They have largely succeeded.

They not only control all that has been discussed thus far (and far beyond that in corporations we know nothing about, that are hiding their identity behind "apparent owners") but they also own stock in thousands of companies and hold controlling powers by the amount of stock they own. Or, by encouraging affiliation with large corporations, other international banks, and multinational corporations abroad, they exercise a powerful influence in what those businesses decide with respect to the coming new world order.

With the leaders of the banking, industrial, and business world of Japan tied in with them, they can control much of what goes on in the ultimate development of the Far East, and are now doing so.

The international banking families are deeply dug into the European scene, along with the United States of America, Canada, New Zealand, Australia, and Japan.

If the hardy, antigovernment-minded people of Australia knew that their government did not own and operate their money-printing system, and that it was instead, operated, and directed by foreigners in the international banking community, I believe they would rise up in force and get rid of it, one way or another.

What many people of Canada do not know is that the Reserve Bank of Canada is run by the international banking community, and that *they* determine (as in New Zealand, the U.S.A., and many countries of Europe) how much money is printed (affecting inflation in each country directly) and what the going interest rates will be for borrowing money at the prime and secondary level. (Prime level means from the country's Reserve Bank to the domestic banks. Secondary level means the price business and you and I have to pay in order to borrow money from the banks locally.)

Much of the money for these nations is printed in the original international banking country of England, by two or three companies operating in conjunction with the individual governments. Everything has to be ratified by the individual governments—that is what makes it so uncanny! Why would they do such a thing? The reason is that they "do not know how to handle the economy," they were told over and over again, and that the economy needed to be left to the "monetary experts" to control the printing and flow of money and the final determination of interest rates for loans and bonds for each country.

Over the years these international banking conglomerates convinced government after government that they could do the job for them, as they have been doing so successfully in many countries of the world. They were sitting on the doorsteps of the new countries as soon as they were born.

One of the major companies producing money for the new and old countries is the De la Rue Company in England, which produces currencies for over 70 countries of the world.

In Canada, the Bank of Canada is privately owned and operated. It is not owned by the Canadian government. It is exactly as its counterpart in the United States, the Federal Reserve System. (This system took years to establish in the beginning, for many senators and presents saw through the swindle in the U.S.A.)

The Open Market Committee

When the "Open Market Committee" meets every three weeks in Washington, they determine what the interest rates will be and what the flow of money will be for that month. Members of the Federal Reserve Board (appointed by the President) are present and vote, but they have little banking experience in some cases, and are out maneuvered by the banking officials of the Federal Reserve Banks. Five presidents of Federal Reserve Banks sit on this committee, which has such tremendously important powers affecting the people of the country. How can these men, whose banking income will be vastly affected by their own decisions, vote against their own interests? Would you? That Open Market Committee is weighted with prejudiced interests against the best interests of the people of the United States, and should be abolished or else have its personnel changed.

But the people don't know this in each country where inflation is rapidly rising. The people don't know when the interest rates are high for the prime lending rate, investors will very often invest in government bonds and secure for themselves a higher rate of interest, rather than put the money into the development of the private sector of the economy for the good of all. Right now government bonds are attracting the largest share of American investment money. The money is turned over to the banks (as is all money), and then the banking establishment, operating on the Fractional Reserve System, can make millions in profits for themselves by multiplying the usage of money seven times over. They create something that in reality does not exist. They loan out this nonexisting creation and make unbelievable amounts of interest money on it. They do this in New Zealand, Australia, Canada, and virtually every nation in free Europe!

Talk about who controls and produces inflation! There

is a dual answer in every country. It is not the people; it is not big business with its wage-and-price spirals. (In most cases we have these spirals just to keep up with inflation—not produce it.)

INFLATION IS PRODUCED BY THE BIG SPENDING BUDGETS OF GOVERNMENTS IN HARMONY WITH THE BIG BANKING ESTABLISHMENT CONTROLLING THE FLOW OF MONEY AND INTEREST RATES.

If we could curtail government budgets and make governments live within their incomes (taxes), and stop the foreign powers controlling the money creation, interest creation, etc., by turning this power over to government economists and legislators under the strictest government control and supervision and monitoring, we could stop inflation in every country of the world, establish wages and prices at a normal level for each country's economy, and increase employment, production, manufacturing, and business in every part of the international marketplace.

Money production must grow only at the rate of the GNP of each country. If the Gross National Product of any given country is 4 percent, then the money flow should only be growing at a maximum of 5 or 6 percent in order to insure the existence of enough money to keep in circulation the goods and services produced by the GNP.

Money that is produced faster by any commercial bank or Federal Reserve Bank, as in the U.S. or by any Reserve Bank in any of the countries named, is inflationary money and must of necessity cause all prices in that country to rise correspondingly. Citizens-consumers feel that inflation is simply higher prices for everything needed. High prices reflect government-produced inflation. Inflation is really an "inflation of the nation's currency to a damaging degree." Higher prices are the effects of inflation.

Wage-and-price spirals as they continue in many countries of the Western world (including Israel as an important industrial nation, though tiny) follow inflation of the currency.

The Reasons for Money Expansion

Why inflate the currency of any nation? There are at least three reasons.

1. Government expenditures by the legislators demand more printed money than that which is coming into the government via taxes. It is called "monetization of the government debt." This money always winds up back in the economy (via the government to the banks) and creates a situation in which there is too much money for the goods and services in the land. Thus there is a rise in the prices of goods and services. There are good and bad reasons for government debts. Governments have their budget to meet and monetize. So in establishing the government fiscal budget, they *determine how* much extra money they will need from their Reserve Banks in any given country, and then, over and above the estimated tax revenue, they order bonds to be printed and sold to the Reserve Banks (with interest, of course—usually fairly high). The Reserve Bank takes the bonds printed by the government and gives the government the credit or cash money they require for the government budget.

THE BIGGER THE BUDGET, THE LARGER THE AMOUNT OF MONEY THAT MUST BE PRINTED BY THE FED.

When politicians promise many social services to the people in order to get into office (as all presidents and legislators do), and when these promises become law as a result of votes and/or commitments kept, the budget goes up. If we adopt a universally accepted medical-hospital plan in the U.S. (as presented by the President or Senator Kennedy, for instance), the costs of government spending will soar. All additional costs will not be covered by the incoming taxes or the windfall energy profit tax. Consequently the printing presses will run. Many government items on the budget are absolutely necessary, such as defense, certain areas of welfare, energy expenses, etc. But much of what the government gets into it ought not to. Subsidies to large companies that cannot make it on their own should be dropped. Let the astute businessman and the general marketplace determine who stays in business and who doesn't. When governments borrow from Central Banks, they pay interest TO THE OWNERS of the Reserve Banks.

Government grants, giveaways, and wasteful spending (as in the case of the proven waste and inefficiency of the General Services Administration) represent millions of dollars gone down the tubes. There are unending increases in bureaucratic spending for committees to spend more money on examination, investigations, and regulations. The last thing we need in America is more committees to regulate the marketplace for the people! The truth of the matter is that the people will regulate the marketplace beautifully. They have proven in times gone by that they are a much more dependable source of stabilization of wages and prices than wasteful government bureaucrats.

2. The second reason for expanding the money supply is pure greed by the controlling hands of the international bankers, who know that when they run the presses for different countries at different times they are producing terrible inflation. This in turn causes destabilization of wages and prices and throws everything into economic tailspins. Again we go back to the time-proven theory that has worked in history over and over again—print only one or two percent more money than the gross national product of the country. This will produce the only balance needed between supply and demand in order to keep goods and services in circulation.

But the big boys know that when they turn the presses on, eventually inflation will injure general business. Certain businesses will not be able to make it, especially if the banks who made loans to those businesses call in the loans at a time when the owners cannot meet all the payment schedules. What happens then? The banks can foreclose and seize a portion (if not all) of the business. That man is out of the marketplace, and the banks own the newly acquired business and can sell it for a profit or add it to their constantly growing assets.

The international bankers controlling the inflation in any given country can then also inflate the economy by the Fractional Reserve System existing in that country. By creating something out of nothing, they can earn millions in interest payments on money that does not exist.

By overheating the economy this way—by turning on the presses and printing much money, and by using the Fractional Reserve System and other inflationary powers they possess—banks will impose a high interest rate on the use of the money through their persuasion and powers, as in the case of the Open Market Committee in the U.S. This puts much printed money and credit money on the market, but makes it unavailable for the private sector, in many cases. A businessman who needs more money for expansion of his production facilities cannot afford to borrow the money at the going high interest rates. Thus he cuts back on production and lays off employees. This is happening the world over today because of inflation. A world wide recession is on the way.

But in the money-investment area, big investors will invest in the high-rated government bonds and high-interest-yielding Reserve Banks rather than in the commercial sector of the country. This curtails development of the country, but puts much money into the hands of the bankers, and the process begins all over again with the Fractional Reserve System: You invest in the banks, they create more money out of thin air and loan it out for interest (on nothing) and make more and more money on your interest and principal payments as they come in—all from nothing! But they are getting rich!

3. The third reason for turning on the printing presses

with government authorization and cooperation is the need of wartime supplies and equipment.

If war is looming on the horizon, on go the presses to print the money to buy the weapons, make the weapons, and pay the soldiers, along with equipping them, feeding them, and transporting them. War is costly, especially nuclear war. It is costly in precious lives, it is costly and beyond imagination in terms of dollars.

The international bankers are obviously happy about war. It causes more money to be printed and thus more government bonds with interest in exchange for dollars printed for them—unbelievable wealth being paid for by the citizens of that country through taxation.

The bankers know they have subsidiary companies that will supply the weapons, many for the necessities of war for *all nations involved*.

They will finance both sides! They plan on making a complete economic killing out of this next world war—the greatest profit ever. Their sons do not fight, nor do they. Their money is not paying taxes. It is safe in "trust havens."

Out of World War Three, though millions will die in this oil war, some will become unbelievably rich and internationally powerful to the extent of controlling all sources of energy, food, and money. As Dr. Henry Kissinger once said, "Whoever controls these, controls the world."

Summing It All Up

Those who control the flow of money to the country and to the government will continue printing freely weekly.

Mr. Paul Volcker, appointed by the President to the position of Chairman of the Federal Reserve Board, has been known for many years as a liberal when it comes to the printing presses.

He sounds conservative, but his past record assures us of his continued position against a gold-backed dollar. He worked feverishly for demonetization of gold, and he won.

He is against gold in the role of the monetary. He will work against it, but not successfully. Over the past 6000 years gold has weathered bigger storms than Volcker can throw at it.

He will be in favor of printing excessively, which will be inflationary for the country and a tragedy for the dollar. This will precipitate higher fuel prices from the Arabs, as they hike up the prices of oil again and again over the next few years in an attempt to gain rather than lose money on a barrel of oil.

All of this will hit the American public hard in the money belt. Tough times are ahead economically for all of us. While they give us more money in the money supply, they will tighten credit and make money very expensive, as now, with the exorbitant prime interest rate.

By making money expensive to borrow, they cut production in the country and stagnate business. Thus we will have and do have a diminishing GNP now, and it will get worse, causing layoffs, cutbacks, and unemployment statistics to rise terribly, along with inflation.

Is all this planned? Is this a contrived war that is ahead? Are we being conspiratorily plunged into a deep recession and then a planned depression? I BELIEVE SO.

Chapter 7
I Predict

I base the predictions in this chapter not just on gut feelings, but on personal knowledge of many areas of the world. Some of these predictions are not hard for me, because of my world travels and my experiences in these lands, and also because of my complete faith in the Biblical predictions concerning these lands and peoples. Here is what I predicted in the past.

1. I predicted that the Jews would return to the land. They did in 1948.

2. I predicted the phenomenal rise of industry and of military powers in Russia in the 1950s, when they had nothing.

3. I predicted the continuing animosity of the Arabs against Israel. (Not a hard one!)

4. I predicted the shortage of energy in America and of natural resources. It has happened.

5. I predicted the losses in real estate that happened in the recession of the early seventies.

6. I predicted the great rise in the price of gold. Even as far back as 1973, I predicted the price of $300 to $500 per ounce.

7. I predicted the great rise in the price of silver. It has already topped my prediction!

8. I predicted bank failures in the seventies that we did not have in the sixties. We have had them!

9. I predicted a recession for 1979 and a great slipping of the GNP for 1979. It has happened and is increasing into the 1980s.

10. I predicted real estate prices slipping in pocket areas around the country. It is happening now.

11. I predicted that food costs would double in five years, and they did from 1974 to 1979. In some cases they increased more than that!

12. I predicted higher unemployment when President Carter took office.

13. I predicted gasoline at a dollar or more a gallon when we were still in the 50 cent and 60 cent bracket for gas.

14. I predicted that Lebanon one day would fall into a pro-Soviet position against Israel's best interest. It has taken place.

15. I predicted that Iran would turn against Israel. U.S. history bore me out in 1979.

16. I predicted that all of ancient Persia (Iran, Iraq, Afghanistan, Syria, Jordan, Saudia Arabia, Turkey, etc.) would turn totally anti-Israel, anti-U.S.A. and pro-Russia. That most of this has happened we all know. Turkey is last on the list.

17. I predicted that Ethiopia and Somalia and Yemen and Libya would turn anti-Israel, anti-U.S.A., and pro-Soviet. They have done so and/or doing so in these areas.

18. I predicted that the European Common Market would take in a tenth nation, (Greece).

19. I predicted that Russian and Chinese Communist forces would not fight one another.

20. I predicted that the Soviets would gain control of the Cape of Good Hope trade routes for Western ships. This has not happened yet. I hope it won't.

21. I predicted the nonrise of the stock market. It should be at 1800 to 1900 on the DJI just to keep up with the inflation of the seventies. It is in the low 800s now.

22. I predicted that the gas shortages on the mainland of the U.S. would be proved contrived, and that they would be used to hike gasoline prices even further. That came true.

Well, so much for my successes of the past. I only mentioned them to establish myself in your mind.

Foolish and speculative predictions would do nothing for my credibility and respectability where you and the public are concerned, so cautiously and respectfully I make the following predictions for various realms of life.

Assuming that my understanding of certain biblical prophecies is correct, and that my timing for their fulfillment is accurate, along with my understanding of economics, geography, sociology, military alliances, and politics, then as the pieces of the giant global puzzle come together for the SOCIALIZED, ONE—WORLD GOVERNMENT TO TAKE PLACE, THE FOLLOWING PREDICTIONS WILL AFFECT YOU AND YOUR FAMILY AND FRIENDS AND ASSOCIATES DRASTICALLY.

POLITICAL AND MILITARY PREDICTIONS AFFECTING THE ENTIRE GLOBE

1. As Egypt opens her borders through the Suez Canal to Israel and vice versa, Jordan will start to close hers with Israel, in readiness for Soviet-Arab war against the State of Israel in the decade of the 1980s.
2. Many attempts to assassinate President Sadat will take place.
3. Egypt will not join the Arab forces against Israel unless Sadat is murdered. She will remain an Arab neutral.
4. Yasser Arafat and Moamar Gaddafi of Libya will stir up the Arab nations with Saudi Arabian support to "liberate Jerusalem."
5. All Arab OPEC states will join in this prewar rhetoric.
6. Christian forces in Lebanon, friendly to Israel and supplied now by Israel, will fail to control the country.
7. Syrian-backed PLO forces will take Lebanon completely, with Soviet blessings and armament.
8. King Hussein will take an increasingly hard stance against his former distant friend Israel. He will close the

borders at first temporarily and then permanently as a gesture of ill will against Israel, unless the PLO feel this is the way to infiltrate and wreak havoc in Israel.

9. Former feuding Arab factions will join together, forgetting their feuds, and will form the Arab Legion of old in a holy war against the Zionists.

10. Turkey, because of her problems with Greece (a non-Moslem nation of non-Arabs) her Moslem ties with the Arab world, and her close proximity to the Soviet Union, will swing more and more anti-American, pro-Soviet, and pro-Arab. She will eventually join the Arab-Moslem holy war against Israel, backed by the Soviets. Iran will prove to be the lit fuse, eventually exploding in all of the Mideast and Turkey.

11. As a result of this decision, Turkey, who is hurting in her economy, will get much oil money to aid her and many Soviet supplies to assist her through the perils of rampant inflation and economic hardships for her people.

12. Certain African nations that are now Moslem in their beliefs will fight with the Arabs and will politically align themselves with the Arab world against Israel and against the U.S. interests in the Middle East.

13. All North African Arab states (Moslem) will join in the alliance against Israel with the rest of the Arab world —Morocco, Algeria, and Libya. Only Egypt will abstain, as long as President Sadat survives. How long can he survive? My prayers are for his long life. He is a good man.

14. We will now see much military shipping coming from the Soviet Union through the Bosporus (Istanbul) into the Sea of Marmara into the Aegean Sea, emptying into the Mediterranean Sea in preparation for the war.

15. Cyprus will become a Soviet naval base, along with increasing development of the Libyan naval base occupied by the USSR.

16. Bolstered by its apparent success at pressuring the white powers of Rhodesia into securing a black government there, the U.S.A. will continue (as long as President Carter is

in the picture) to pressure South African white powers into a black government there. The net result will be increasing Soviet involvement by infiltration and stirring up of the blacks. We could lose South Africa as America's friend.

17. The greatest arms buildup in world history will be seen immediately in the Middle East—greater than in recent years (and that has been unprecedented).

18. Negotiations for peace with the Israelis and Arabs via the U.S.A. and U.S.S.R. negotiators will break down in confusion, and ultimately will end in walkouts and terrible disputes.

19. The United States will pour billions more dollars than planned into Israel to protect her, so that the U.S. will have a springboard for action against the Arabs and Russians if a war breaks out. The State of Israel is the only country that is friendly to U.S. interests in the Middle East now. We need Israel as much as she needs us.

20. There will be a great slowing down in the production of oil in the OPEC cartel, in order to reinforce the demands of the Arabs against Israel. This will affect the whole world at first, and especially the U.S.

21. Nations dependent on OPEC oil (as in the case of Japan, etc.) will declare their immediate allegiance to the Arabs.

22. The U.S. will not be able to switch from the Jewish to the Arab side because of long-term commitments to Israel and because of the historic link between the two countries politically and religiously.

23. Most European nations will favor the Arab position because of their need of oil supplies.

24. It's hard to say what the Dutch will do this time, but if I am allowed a guess, they will stick to the Israelis again. The Dutch don't forget alliances easily, nor are they as intimidated by the oil situation as others are.

25. In principle Canada will remain on the side of the U.S.—with Israel, against the war, and against the boycott.

26. Canada will sell more and more oil to the U.S.A. in

the pinch. Their prime minister will have many storms in Parliament over this issue!

27. Mexico will produce more and will help fill the oil gap caused by the Arabs in the U.S.A.

28. I look for Australia and New Zealand to try to be neutral, but because their oil supplies come from the OPEC cartel, eventually they will capitulate to the Arab pressure.

29. The Soviets, after things cool down some in Iran, will exercise great respect and caution for the new regime. The net result will be many Soviet technicians in Iran working in the oil fields, as in Iraq now. They want the oil.

30. Russia will help Turkey——economically and with military grants.

31. China will stay out of the whole thing completely!

32. China will build her industries quietly with Japanese, European, American, and Canadian aid while the war preparations go on. She will await the results with glee, hoping for the demise of the Soviet Union through it all.

33. China will remain politically on the side of the Western nations, providing all her own oil needs and perhaps some for export to the U.S. if needed at this time.

34. China and Japan will exchange goods, science and services to an extent that has been unparalleled in the two countries.

35. The Japanese economy will grow tremendously in the next five years as she sells unbelievable amounts of goods and services to mainland China. Japan will be strong.

36. Investments in certain products in Japan will bring a tremendous return for your money in the next five years. If you are in a position to invest, have your broker make a check on the latest contracts and pending contracts for Japan to supply China, such as durable goods. It looks terrific for the durable goods market and for big investments to make big money! It'll beat anything made here.

37. The Japanese industrial might and economic development will exceed that of the U.S.A. per capita.

38. The European Gross National Product is going to slip from what it has been. Europe needs a dynamic leader to take over the Western nations and fuse them into a working unit of power instead of 9 or 10 nations struggling to do it through the Common Market alone.

39. The 9 nations will soon become 10 nations of the European Confederacy.

40. Greece will be the tenth to join on the executive level of the EEC.

41. The 10 nations of EEC will use their own European money, the ECU (European Currency Unit), to great advantage with the oil nations and against the interests of the dollar in the 1980s. My book HOW TO SURVIVE THE MONEY CRASH explains the use and creation of ECU.

42. The 10 nations of the European Community will select a dynamic, charismatic leader to unify Europe and bring about an equitable economy in all 10 nations and greater stability within the market.

43. Three of the 10 nations in the European Market will resist this world leader and his associates (another biblical prediction for you to check out—Daniel 7;7-24.

44. Saudi Arabia will declare war on Israel after the talks fail to produce a change.

45. The Saudis will pressure the U.S.A. to pressure Israel into giving up the city of Jerusalem and the West Bank, or else the oil will be cut off.

46. Preparations for the war will begin shortly thereafter in the U.S.A., with a new President who "isn't going to take the Arab guff anymore!"

47. The actual war in the Middle East involving America will be preceded by drastic cutbacks in the economy and a resultant slowing of the GNP beyond any expectation of the government economists and the public.

ECONOMIC PREDICTIONS FOR THE U.S.A. AND THE WORLD, PRIOR TO WAR

48. The worst of tight interest rates (affecting the prime and secondary loan rates to all) will last until just before the election. This will be government and FED action to curtial inflation, but it will fuel unemployment.

49. There will be tragic increasing unemployment.

50. There will be a surprise by the government for the people—a burst of government to create jobs in the private and government sectors for the unemployed of the nation. This bubble will break after the inauguration of the new president.

51. The only way Mr. Carter will be reelected will be to pull this plum out the government's economic pie for the man on the street. If Carter can pull it off, then he may make it. But the general dissatisfaction with this leader today makes me doubt that he will make it.

53. Kennedy *could* become President, unless he feels his ascendancy to that position will bring his death, as it did for his brothers.

54. If you are reading this book after the elections, then you have started reading this book right in the heat of the fulfillments—the most exciting time to understand these prophecies. Watch closely as they happen!

54. In the general slowdown of America's economy, many large and small manufacturers and retailers of durable goods will cut back tremendously, and great layoffs will result.

55. Many business bankruptcies will appear on the economic horizon as you are reading this book.

56. There will be cutbacks in housing, and in all the related industries of the housing world—kitchen and bathroom appliances as well as heating, air-conditioning,

electrical, and plumbing supplies. Tradesmen will be out of work, and there will be a general slump in the building industries.

57. New-car sales will slump—for large cars in particular.

58. Trades dealing with used cars will flourish.

59. Used appliances sales will flourish. Consider it as a business.

60. Television sales should be good, along with radios, as many people will use these for entertainment as they cut back other entertainments for economic reasons.

61. Gold sales will soar as gold rises in value and the dollar dips, along with the general economy. As prices go down for homes and stocks, many more people will turn to gold.

62. Silver sales will soar, as will the value of silver coins. You should have some silver (and gold, of course) if you don't already. Silver and gold are still great for investments, as hedges against inflation, and for SURVIVAL in a world that still loves those two precious metals far above government-issued currencies.

63. The value of diamonds and other precious stones and gems will soar in value. Even the cost of the gold and silver and platinum in their mountings will cause the rise, to say nothing of having the stones themselves. They are not easy to resell, however.

64. Small cars will rise in price fast. Demand will determine this. Gas is the reason, of course—not comfort. We will be sacrificing style and comfort for economy, and rightly so.

65. More and more people will think of farming communities as they think about safety and food and quietness with which to live and raise their families. A very wise move indeed. You can find a job in a smaller area if you look for it.

66. Hospital costs (and thus insurance costs) will soar.

67. Auto insurance is soaring and will continue to do so as repairs and .parts cost more because of increasing labor costs and energy costs.

68. More people will be buying smaller cars and used cars to save on the insurance costs as well as on energy.

69. Many people will be forced to sell their cars, trucks, boats, and recreation vehicles, and to turn instead to public transportation where it is available.

70. One of the worst businesses to be in will be the recreational vehicle business. It is already suffering badly.

71. Resort areas are going to suffer, and some will go completely out of business. Hawaii will be the last to suffer.

72. Where it takes long-distance driving, ski resorts, summer resorts, and gambling areas will all suffer incredibly.

73. Housing in these areas will be the first to hit the market at the lowest prices in the nation. This includes Lake Tahoe, Reno, Las Vegas, and Mammoth Mountain —these in particular because of the long driving distances. You will be able to buy a condo or home in these areas cheaper than anywhere else in the nation.

74. Ski resorts in Utah won't suffer much, nor near Denver, because they have large cities nearby to fuel the business. Skiing at Big Bear in Southern California will be at an all-time high. People won't have to drive too far, and they can easily have gas left over after the return trip.

75. Industrial cities large and small, like Detroit, Chicago, New York, Philadelphia, Los Angeles, Youngstown, Cleveland, Pittsburgh, Baltimore, Akron, Buffalo and Cincinnati will all be hit very hard with disastrous layoffs, unemployment, welfare payments, and crime.

76. Agricultural cities will fare much better. Farmers will get the oil they need, and the government will make sure that food is produced in abundance.

77. Oil cities, as in Texas, should boom and not feel

the pinch too much. Much of the industry is oil-related and will be in full swing.

78. Cities depending on air-conditioning to make them livable, like Phoenix, Palm Springs, Tucson, etc. will be hit hard. Energy shortages will cause many to suffer in the South because of the extreme heat. Others will suffer in the Northeast for a lack of heat in the winter—more than in any winter of the seventies. The people are not ready for such deprivation.

79. This generation does not have the patience or the understanding to put up with things that their parents and grandparents did. Thus rising crime rates everywhere are blowing the minds of the law-enforcement officials. Never before in our history have we had the lawlessness we are going to see in the decade of the eighties.

80. The worst place for you to live with your family as the eighties deepen is in the big cities. Crime will have a much better opportunity to strike you, if you stay.

81. Multiracial cities will be hit the hardest. Races tend to blame other races for the local problems. Be a sobering influence for good as you have opportunity.

82. Small farming communities, from 10,000 to 30,000 population, are the places to live. They are not dependent on outside industries for salaries, jobs, or food. They can support themselves. Find such a community and live there, even if the pace is slower and the sidewalks fold up at 7 p.m. Enjoy more natural pursuits for personal pleasure, instead of the artificial. There are many wonderful things that God has given us to enjoy, but we ignore them until we want peace of mind.

Have you strolled down a country lane lately? Have you smelled the fresh hay after harvest? How about a simple picnic? Or must you have the sophisticated restaurants every time? A little boat ride on a country river or on a nearby pond, gathering food out of your own garden—it sounds like heaven! But you can have it. May this book inspire you to get it. Don't buy it—just lease or rent it! This is not the time to tie up your money in buying ventures. Later, if you wish (and we all have time) you will be able to buy blocks of houses with your gold and silver!

83. You know this one: food is going sky-high! Buy extra dehydrated things now. Buy some extra suplies and store them now. At today's prices they will seem like a bargain to you six months from now! Write me for the free information on how to buy these things.

84. Large luxury items will not be selling. Get out of retailing those items (pools, boats, vans, etc.)

85. We are going to see less and less variety of goods for sale, and more "sales" going on, as retailers sell off inventories and think twice about buying new styles and kinds.

86. Every industry is going to feel the pinch—steel, lumber, autos, shipping, flying, transportations, entertainment, stock market, travel, etc.

87. The only industry not suffering as much as others will be the food industry. Though I see high-class and high-priced restaurants out of business in some areas. Many people who now eat out and think nothing of it will soon reconsider.

88. I look for book sales and related industries to do well. Publishers should do fairly well compared to other industries. People are reading more. As things get worse, books will get cheaper and will always be a good way to make a living, as I see it. People always want some form of entertainment. Books will be the cheapest and the finest at the time. They provide endless hours of escape from reality into a world of fun, exciting times, and faraway places.

89. Birthrates will increase in the Western Nations, along with the sale of contraceptives. People will have more time on their hands for sex, affection, and general living. Those concerned will buy contraceptives.

90. Evening time, pastimes, games of chance, and fun

with skilled games will take up more time and will be selling well.

91. Many churches will experience tremendous growth. People are turning to God and religion as never before. As times get tough and fear fills hearts, many will turn to faith in God.

92. Speaking of fear, there will be unprecedented numbers of people taking their own lives in suicide. Pressure will bring this on soon. It will accelerate as the changing times bring more pressure and less pleasure.

93. Psychiatric and general hospitals will have a larger patient load than now, with psychosomatic illnesses up by a large number. People will not be able to cope with the changes for the worse: loss of jobs, security, homes, cars, etc.

94. Those in the field of health care will prosper and be very busy, never out of work, including doctors, nurses, dentists, counselors, psychiatrists, and assistants to these fields. This also applies to the support industries of drugs and pharmaceuticals.

95. Drug addiction will increase throughout the nations mentioned in this book. Crime will increase to support the habits to an unparalleled degree.

96. The military draft will be reinstated. Many people will parade against it, but it will go through for national security reasons.

97. The greatest resort city in America—Honolulu— will suffer greatly because people will not have the money to fly there in the mid-eighties. Condominium sales will drop in Hawaii, and prices will ultimately come down.

98. New Zealand and Australia will not suffer initially as badly as the U.S.A. and Canada. These two nations will have a setback in their GNP, and with tremendous inflation the people will suffer unemployment. But because they will probably not buck the Arabs, they will get oil.

99. In the 1980s, all Western nations will eventually suffer cutbacks in oil consumption and will thus feel the ef-

fects economically. The U.S. will feel this the most.

100. Canada will suffer along with the United States for several internal and related reasons.

First, her economy has been largely developed by U.S. money, and though much of the industry is run by Canadians, it is for export as well as for domestic consumption. Though Canada may not experience a lack of energy, she will certainly experience a lack of sales for her productions. Her greatest export market, the U.S.A., may not be buying much except oil. There will also be a lack of exports to the U.K. and Europe, as demand will be off there also.

Secondly, Canada is generally so closely related to the economic rises and falls of her neighbor to the south that for the U.S. to have major setbacks and the effect not to be felt in Canada is highly unlikely.

Canada will have the energy to produce. At the beginning of all the trouble, Canada will fare much better than the United States, but as the problems of the eighties deepen, the results of the terrible slowdown in the U.S. will be felt there more and more. Brace yourself, Canadians!

101. Canada is going to be a great place to live if you are self-supporting or a farmer, or if you receive your income from outside Canada during the next few years.

Canada has all the natural resources anyone could want. It has lots of water, much more than the U.S. ever had. There are abundant minerals, from which the U.S. gets much of its needed supplies now. And there is lots of food and good land for those who work hard.

If you have an American income or American money to invest (from the sale of your house, etc.), you could do much worse than to take that money to Canada and live. It will be a great place to live during the eighties. You would receive more for your money in Canada from the dollar, inasmuch as the U.S. dollar buys about 12 to 18 percent more there than in the U.S.

Secondly, housing is priced lower in Canada than in the

U.S., especially in British Columbia, where the rivers are teaming with fish, the snow-capped mountains are high and beautiful, and the people are friendly and speak English! Canada has plenty of food, plenty of oil, plenty of water and plenty of land, but only the population of California—23 million people—in an area larger than the U.S.A.!

102. As the oil shortages hit the industrial centers, real estate values in those cities will sag fast. In all the cities listed under that point, sell now. Don't wait. You will lose your shirt when industry folds up totally or even partially as the oil crunch comes, either through manipulation by the "seven sisters" and/or Saudi Arabia delivering the ultimatum.

103. Real-estate values will plunge lower at first, then pause and plunge again. Look for the steam to go out of the economic boilers when oil shortages hit the industrial centers. Real estate, when it starts, will plunge terribly and inexorably! It is already down in Washington, Houston, Chicago, and California. In the resort areas, I see Tahoe dropping first, Reno second, Las Vegas third, and Florida and Hawaii last. Depending on the airlines, the resort areas will last the longest.

104. Do you want a lovely home, cheap, soon? Look at Reno, where they have overbuilt for the skiing industry, gambling industry, and general pleasure reasons. Here is where you will get your first great bargains. I know, for I have lived there for several years, and I see the diminishing business affecting everything.

105. There will be a great acceleration in the inflation rate for the entire nation (and in other nations, such as New Zealand, Australia, Canada, England, etc.). This inflation will then suddenly heat up into hyperacceleration of the inflation rate.

106. This hyperinflation rate will bring with it the graduating degrees of recession. Recessionary forces are at work now, and will rapidly increase until we have the

counteracting force of a terrible depression in the United States.

107. The only thing bringing this depression sooner than 1984 will be the Saudis delivering the oil ultimatum to us sooner. When they deliver the oil-shutdown message, this will catapult this nation overnight into the economic descent of depression, which will be far worse than 1929-33!

108. We cannot keep on inflating the economy without the drastic results of depression with its high unemployment rate, high crime rate, and unbelievable psychotic behavior of people because they have been accustomed to 35 years of plenty and prosperity. We are not adjusted to sacrifice in America.

109. The president and his press secretary promised an alleviation of the oil shortage the following month. The next news broadcast revealed that Texaco and Gulf ordered less and less gas for the next three months and more! It will be the latter rather than the former promise that will be kept, with its consequences to the slipping economy and growing inflation.

110. Because the U.S. deficit budgeting is allowing for more debts due to imports, and because our import-export ratio is so bad (primarily due to oil imports and their costs), we will see the dollar slip tragically, and costs of all products leap out of bounds. Buy some gold and silver now!

111. It could very well happen that the president will ban taking more than a certain amount of U.S. money out of the country by tourists, and will limit overseas travel. We will see the government embark on a "buy American goods" advertising campaign.

DEPRESSION PREDICTIONS FOR THE FUTURE

112. Over 25 percent of the work force of the United States will be out of work when the depression is at its

height, precipitated either by the Arabs in the oil shutdown or by the constant inflation of the economy and the results of depression as we reach the end of the dollar's value. Either reason could provoke the depression. We can only inflate the dollar so far and so long, and then it snaps with virtual worthlessness. Or the oil shutdown will bring depression sooner than inflation.

113. Workers and professional management staffs in the following industries will be out of work to a large extent: Automotive industry; steel industry; household appliances industry; aerospace industry; housing and building industry; building supply and related service industry; entertainment industry; recreational vehicle industry (boats, RV's, campers); tool and die industry; and many, many more, all of which are related to a working economic order of balance that demands their products in normal times. These will not be normal times.

114. Those who will fare the best and eat the best will be: farmers, who will get special allotments of oil; hospital and medical staffs; insurance personnel; second-hand automotive dealers; auto mechanics; retail and wholesale food outlets; pharmaceutical supplies; certain government agencies, such as police and firemen, as well as local, state, and federal agencies and leaders (we couldn't do without them!). Those Americans who are sharp now will take their savings and sell those pieces of property and items they do not need, and will live where they can be quiet and peaceful with food growing outside and a good supply of water.

115. Government authorities during this depression will set up agencies for feeding the people in every major and minor city, as best as possible. It will be on a one-meal-a-day basis. Look for it first in Detroit, New York, Chicago, and Los Angeles.

116. Rioting, looting, stealing, and rape will be the common news for America. Rape will increase because of desperation over the futility of the situation. Stealing will

be to eat and support drug habits. Much "justified steal-ing" will go on to support families.

117. More people will be buying guns and defensive weapons than ever before!

118. Divorce statistics will rise unbelievably as men leave home for "greener pastures of opportunity."

119. Welfare rolls will increase, burdening the govern-ment to the ultimate with the financial strain.

120. I predict that the government will come out with a NEW KIND OF MONEY. They will drop the American greenback and substitute a type of paper money more like Canada's new money—different colors for different denominations. This will be beautiful money, but it will not be worth more than what we have now, for the govern-ment will not have gold and silver to back it up, nor a GNP to be proud of. This country will be very weak. People will be forced to accept the money, but will be very unhappy about what it will not do for them. It will not end the depression.

121. It will take 10 or more years to struggle out of this depression, with the result that Europe will take the lead economically, politically, and militarily in the world.

The U.S. will be considered second class as a nation from this economic point on . . . unfortunately. Rome has fallen again!

122. Those who bought gold will be the ones surviving the best, along with those holding silver. These people, in-telligent enough to foresee the demise of the dollar through inflation, or what the Arabs could do to us, will be sitting on top of the world, compared to their neighbors and friends who bought none while the going was good. The holders of gold and silver will readily buy food (they pro-bably have much of it stored already) and the necessities of life. Merchants will welcome their money, for it has always proven in a time of crisis to be the real thing.

Many people are holders of the *true gold* as well as of monetary gold, the precious metal. What is true gold? It is knowing Jesus Christ as your personal Savior, as I do. It means that you have bought real gold, awarding you forgiveness of sins in this life, daily divine guidance in all your undertakings and problems, and eternal life in the hereafter! This is quite a deal, when you consider that real gold does not take money to enjoy. It just requires a barter trade of your old sins for Christ's new life. Have you put your faith in Christ and asked Him to forgive your sins? This is where it all begins. It's described in Ephesians 2:1-9.

Chapter 8
How To Survive The Oil War

There are several extremely important considerations when you are thinking and planning SURVIVAL during this crisis period that is coming to the United States, and partially to Canada (because of her dependence on the U.S. for trade and commerce).

1. WHERE TO LIVE FOR SAFETY AND REASONABLE COMFORT.
2. WHAT MATERIALS TO GATHER NOW IN ORDER TO BE ABLE TO EAT THEN.
3. HOW TO MENTALLY PREPARE YOURSELF AND YOUR FAMILY FOR DEPRIVATION.
4. HOW TO PREPARE SPIRITUALLY.

I believe a logical case has been presented supporting the imminency of the coming oil war.

This prediction, and that of the others just considered, you see developing virtually every day in the local newspapers and on the TV news each evening. Generally speaking, things are getting worse every week.

Where to Live

As I have already pointed out, living in or near a large metropolitan city is dangerous in a time of crisis and deprivation, for people turn to violence and thievery to support their needs.

YOU DO WANT TO STAY AWAY FROM:

A. Areas supported primarily by big industry from outside. If the industry closes because of an oil shortage, the area will be especially desolate and deprived.

B. Dependence on air-conditioning for living. Utilities are dependent on oil for producing electricity.

C. Big cities, for their needs will not be supplied. when trucks cannot roll for lack of energy. You will see much violence, food stealing, etc.

D. Resort areas, depending on that area to support you. They are already being hit, and the depression hasn't started yet.

E. Main artery highways, where great amounts of city traffic, looking for food and help, will come your way.

F. Earthquake fault lines, where any sudden cataclysmic upheaval of the elements could wipe you out.

G. Tornado and hurricane territory.

H. Centers of military storage, personnel, and missiles. These could be hit first in a strike from the enemy.

I. Non-food-producing towns. You want to be where the food is.

J. Places far from your work. You may not have fuel to run your car.

YOU DO WANT TO BE IN AN AREA WHERE:

A. People support themselves in food production locally, where food does not have to be trucked or trained in.

B. You are free from tornadoes, cyclones, hurricanes, and earthquakes.

C. There are few military items that the enemy may want to destroy.

D. You have an opportunity to cultivate real friends who act and think like you. You do not have to have many friends—just a few who tick like you.

E. You can store your own food, bottled water, and other survival items without feeling that if you go out for the evening you will be robbed.

F. You can walk down the street in the evening or
    stroll down a country lane in peace with your fami-
    ly, without feeling you are going to be mugged.
G. You can have a large garden.
H. You can store some gasoline drums carefully, safely
    and secretly. Fill them well and don't use them until
    you have to.
I. You will have a good water supply. You may need
    to have a well.
J. You can share your religious beliefs with those of
    "like precious faith."
K. You can find a minister, priest, or rabbi who can
    assist you in times of need and when the pressure is
    on.
L. There are less than 50,000 people. Too many people
    living together can provoke wrath with each other if
    utilities fail due to energy shortages.
M. People are reasonable and not impulsive, arrogant,
    prejudiced, or proud. There are many such places in
    North America.

My Experiences

My wife and I have traveled far and near in the earth and
have found the right and the wrong places to live with
respect to nations and cities. We have found some really
right places to live when all hell breaks loose.

Recently we took a 6000-mile automobile trip just as gas
was short and hard to find.

Florida depends primarily on tourism for support, and
unless you are prepared to live without air conditioning
there when the fuel shortage really hits, and can be totally
self-supporting with an income already arranged or
secured, you would not want to live there.

Some people do not mind the heat in the summer and
can manage without air conditioning. If you are one of
these, and can go to Florida with money in your pocket to
live on, or have an income from business not dependent on

Florida's lack of tourism, then go there.

You will find cheaper living in the Tampa-Saint Petersburg area, and beautiful scenery to bless you daily. If you are a fish-eater and can fish to any extent, you could live very cheaply there with lots of free protein from the sea. In the midst of the crash itself, Florida could be a good place to live *if you can adapt to the above conditions.*

There are small towns and remote regions in Georgia, South Carolina, North Carolina, Tennessee, Kentucky, Ohio, Pennsylvania, and the entire Eastern seaboard that would make lovely, quiet living. But some of them have one of the negatives we mentioned: THEY ARE DEPENDENT ON NORTHERN-RUN FACTORIES TO KEEP THEM ALIVE, BOTH IN THE NORTH AND IN THE SOUTH. Many northern industries have gone South for cheaper labor, etc. This is not the town for you now.

In the Midwest there is lots of room for all of us. Coming through Missouri, Idaho, Nebraska, Wyoming, and Olkahoma, you can find many small towns with their own food and their own supply of water. They raise most of what they need locally, and are not totally dependent on sustenance being brought in.

From what we saw of Utah, you had better leave it to the hardy Mormons. They have done a great job in Salt Lake City. I was impressed indeed. I loved the mountains there and the skiing. They have lots of dehydrated food, as you know, but I do not recommend Utah for the average person.

Nevada is almost in the same category, with the exception of areas in the north, near Oregon, where the land is cultivatable, vast, and really empty. We saw deer everywhere, and cattle all over the highways—plus signs that read "No gas for 75 miles!"

Northern California has some great places to live. You can find small towns, cities, and open spaces galore in spite of the booming metropolis of Los Angeles in the south.

Stay out of the southern area of California. It is headed for trouble.

Everyone there needs a car to move. The city transportation is poor. About 400 cities are back-to-back, and millions of people pollute the air daily and have to be fed by food trucked in, trained in, shipped in, flown in, etc.

Oregon is one of the prime states to live in. You can find towns all over that are small, accommodating, friendly, self-sustaining, noncommercial, green, fresh, and above all, cheaper than most places to rent, lease, and buy.

If you don't mind the rain, Oregon is a great place to live. There are snow, valleys, mountains, water, sunshine, and vegetation galore. Check it out.

One of the prettiest places in all of Oregon is just north of the California line, in Ashland. I nearly pitched my camp there! It looked like the "Sound of Music" and the Swiss Alps combined! Wait till you drive through that area!

Driving on up to Washington you find more of the same—green valleys, high mountains, lots of vegetation, and lots of room for more people who are willing to work and pitch in. It is fabulous terrain for growing, and looks like a marvelous place to live.

My Number One Suggestion

MY NUMBER ONE SUGGESTION TO YOU FOR SERIOUS CONSIDERATON IS JUST NORTH OF WASHINGTON IN BRITISH COLUMBIA, CANADA.

It is, as some people say, "Out of sight!" Nowhere is the scenery more lush or beautiful. There are snow-capped mountains, gorgeous lakes miles long (teeming with all kinds of fish), fruit-filled valleys, productive soil, small towns aplenty, great skiing (water and snow), recreational facilities from tobogganing to ice skating, and snowmobiling, plus comparatively inexpensive homes or apartments to lease or rent. Scores of these areas are totally self-supporting. I have not found a more lovely place to SUR-VIVE.

Canada has its own oil, food, and minerals, plus lots of land, with thousands of lakes filled with every kind of fish imaginable. Canada has friendly people but is not over-populated. You could get lost in British Columbia (in the right sense of that word) easier than anywhere in the world, and make it in a crisis.

You and your family could fish some of those lakes and streams and never run out of food. On half an acre you could plant corn, potatoes, tomatoes, beets, carrots, beans, peas, cucumbers, squash, turnips, lettuce, cabbage, onions, radishes, celery, etc., etc., until you could feed an army.

How do you get into Canada as an American? It's easy. Many Americans own or rent properties in Canada and visit every summer, etc. You can do the same and go there for a period of up to six months without having to im-migrate there. They might not let you in if you tell them you are going to live there permanently. You only plan on temporarily living there anyway. When the problems end or ease somewhat, you will come back to the U.S. In the meantime you go for a visit for a few months, check it out, live here and there if you wish, or in one spot. You can always return over the border for a day and then go back to Canada the same day, reextending your next six-month visa. Actually, the Canadian government is happy to have your money. It helps when you "buy Canadian."

What to Own

There is no better way to hedge against inflation, to be completely prepared for financial emergencies nationally, and to gain money in the world of economic investments today than to own gold and silver bullion or coins.

There is no better way for the average American family to own this insurance money than to buy coins that need no melting, or testing for quality when the rainy day hits, with torrential economic floods upon us, as predicted in this book.

Silver coins are rising phenomenally in value, even faster than gold at this present date of writing.

Gold is moving remarkably and carries with it the mystique of the ages in its intrinsic value. No other metals or kinds of international money carry with them the visions of grandeur that rise up in a man's heart as with silver and gold.

Ask any man with sense if he will accept 500 dollars in any country's currency today or a South African Krugerrand instead, and he will take the gold coin.

Gold is going up every month in the overall picture.

Dollars, francs, pesos, guilders, marks, rubles, rupees, lira, pounds, etc. are all going down steadily in purchasing power. They are being forced down.

For the most part they are not backed by gold or silver. This makes government-issued paper money not as valuable and far more flexible in prices—not nearly as acceptable to other nations as when the money was backed by gold.

Instead, the money is backed by the gross national product. When this GNP falls and the balance of payments gets further and further in the red as governments spend more, buy more, import more, and export less (as in the case of the U.S.A.), the money is worth much less.

Then add the fact that currencies are being too heavily printed by the Reserve Banks, and you have too much currency in each country and not enough gold or goods and services to back it up.

So until we rise up simultaneously and withhold our taxes, or until some brilliant leaders arise in the world to lead us back to the full free-enterprise system that we were founded on (and still possess to some degree), we may have to do other things individually.

First, vote right. Find out about your candidate by writing him and asking what he believes about certain issues that we have discussed in this book. Tell him that if he works for what is right for America, you will personally try to get voters to back him up at the polls.

Pray for a change that will bring about what Americans want and need in order to be the first country in leadership in the world again.

God answers prayers. Then put legs on your prayers and work for this. We are worth saving as country. . . . Don't you agree? We want our children to enjoy this great nation as we did.

Set up a committee in your local school or civic organization to investigate some of the things I have presented in this book, and to get people to understand the issues facing the country. I am convinced that if Americans knew what was behind the troubles and the lack of leadership in Washington, they would do something about it. . . . They would do plenty about it!

But most people just do not know. Could you help in your community to inform, educate, and inspire others to join the team to bring the nation back? Yes, you can.

While you are doing this, store food and water plus kitchen, bathroom, and bedroom necessities somewhere for safety, security, and peace of mind until we win politically or have to go through the tribulation of the days ahead.

Make a game of this one night with the whole family. The theme is: WHAT DO WE NEED AS A FAMILY IF EVERYTHING THE GOVERNMENT SUPPLIES IS TURNED OFF AND VIOLENCE BREAKS LOOSE EVERYWHERE?

Get pads and pencils, and turn the family loose for the most innovative night you have spent in a long time!

Each family member writes down what he or she would need for a two-year period of isolation, deprivation, and segregation from society.

You will find that most water-preserved foods (canned) last two years. Dehydrated foods last ten years and take much less room to store, ship, and travel with. They weigh much less (important if you are shipping by car to a retreat) and are easy to handle and prepare. They also take up much less room if you stay home and store food right where you presently live. Store the food under the bed, in the closet, or up in the attic, but store it away from prying eyes.

Hundreds of thousands of Americans are storing dehydrated and freeze-dried foods, bottled water, and auxiliary cooking facilities (as for camping). Flour, sugar, tea, coffee, milk, beans, and everything dehydratable or freezable is being stored.

Secure a simple retreat in the mountains, valleys, small town, or small city, and stash it full of food, water, blankets, firewood, medicines, prescriptions, toiletries, kitchen aids, utensils, soaps, towels, pots, dishes, etc. Include matches, radios, bicycles, motorbikes, snowmobiles, four-wheelers, guns, ammunition, water supply, gas and oil, boots, blankets, clothes, books, and games. Try to locate near running waters (as in streams, lakes, rivers, etc.) for fishing, sports, and water needs.

We are planning the same. My family will be prepared for the four seasons, and hopefully we will have all of the above and will be able to ski in the winter, swim in the summer, and walk in the woods in the spring and fall, enjoying what the good Lord intended us to enjoy—His creation!

I want to be where I can continue writing, teaching, and reaching people with what's going on in the world, and being a help to all that I can reach. We have our place picked out. Have you?

Remember that you do not have to *buy* one of these retreats. You can rent or lease (with an option to buy).

But start storing now. *If you don't know where to buy gold, silver, food, and provisions, fill in the coupon at the end of the book and we will help you find it all.*

By buying in bulk where your retreat is, you can save

money as you purchase cases, bulk foods, and larger amounts for storage.

A vacation NOW to the spot, making it a "work vacation," will give you encouragement and lots of family fun.

My mentioning of gun and ammunition is in no way to imply that you would kill someone. But if you or your family are attacked, you would certainly use it to warn the attacker. Failing at that, you would wound your adversary sufficiently to keep him from coming back. I am not of the opinion that killing another human being is the answer in any of these situations.

If someone attacks you viciously with intent to kill you, that is another story. You *may* have to aim to kill, but maybe wounding would do the job. In my case, it would have to.

But if someone knocks on your door for food and help, are you going to turn him away unfed? Would you shoot him or her? Certainly not.

We are going to have to feed them and then encourage them to find other green pastures. You can't take in the world, but you should at least be prepared to be a *friend*.

ONE OF THE BIGGEST THINGS YOU CAN DO TO PREPARE YOURSELF FOR THE COMING CALAMITY—THE COMING OIL WAR—IS TO BUY GOLD COINS NOW.

Why? Because when the dollar dies in your country (or whatever currency you are using, wherever you are reading this book), you will want a purchasing unit that is alive and recognized internationally, in case you are traveling.

For illustration's sake, let's assume the oil embargo is on and we are headed for World War Three. There are terrible shortages and tragic crime rates. There is anarchy in the cities, with many people out of work. Panic buying empties stores; city officials are in panic; local governments are unable to handle the people. You have just landed at your retreat safely with the family or friends you have planned this with.

The next news you hear, apart from impending war, is about the value of the dollar. Credibility in the government is almost totally gone. "They let this happen," will be the theme; "the dollar is dying."

Confidence in anything the government produces is almost gone. Inflation is rampant. There are terrible prices everywhere for foods, gas, and other necessities. Everyone is screaming! The dollar's purchasing power is so bad it takes hundreds of dollars to buy a couple of bags of groceries, when you can find a store with any!

Gasoline is up to 20 dollars per gallon, if there is any to be gotten. (You were smart and had some extra stashed away for the proposed trip.)

The stock-market news is unbelievable! Businesses have collapsed. Bankruptcies are announced on the hour. "The market has closed temporarily until adjustments can be made." On Wall Street there is pandemonium day after day during the first month.

Government officials are blaming each other's party. Special congressional meetings are being held into the night in order to return order to the country, solvency to the government, and stability to the dollar. But to no avail. No plan is working.

You have arrived safely in all of this, with your family. You are now safe in the cabin. It is not an auspicious place in these protective mountains, but there was a good dirt road in, you are a long way from the turmoil, the children are planning their first trip to the water shortly, and you and your wife are watching the news on cable TV.

"IT ISN'T GETTING ANY BETTER, LADIES AND GENTLEMEN," says the announcer.

The News

"RIOTS HAVE BROKEN OUT IN EVERY MAJOR CITY THIS WEEK. LOS ANGELES, DETROIT, AND NEW YORK ARE HIT WITH RACIAL VIOLENCE, WITH THE HAVE-NOTS DESTROYING THE HOMES

OF THE HAVES. BEVERLY HILLS WAS SO BADLY
HIT WITH RIOTERS AND LOOTERS THAT THE NA-
TIONAL GUARD WAS CALLED OUT. THE RIOTERS
HIT THE WEALTHIEST AREAS FIRST, WITH GUNS
AND KNIVES. CROWBARS AND SLEDGE HAM-
MERS WERE SEEN AS HOMES WERE BROKEN IN-
TO. THE CELEBRITIES HAVE LONG SINCE GONE
TO RESORTS, AND PLACES OF RETREAT. THE
POLICE ARE HELPLESS TO HOLD THE LOOTERS
BACK. IT LOOKS LIKE WAR ZONE, WITH HOMES
BURNING AND THE NATIONAL GUARD OUT
EVERYWHERE. IF THIS FAILS, THE PRESIDENT
WILL HAVE TO CALL OUT THE ARMED FORCES
TO POLICE THE NATION, AND WE ALL WONDER
HOW MUCH GOOD THAT WILL DO.

"WE REALLY ENCOURAGE ALL OF YOU TO
JOIN RELATIVES AND MAKE SURE YOUR HOUSES
ARE SECURELY LOCKED AND THAT YOU ARE
ARMED. WE TAKE GREAT DISPLEASURE AT THIS
ANNOUNCEMENT, BUT THERE IS NO OTHER
ALTERNATIVE, BECAUSE OUR POLICING OF-
FICIALS ARE SO BUSY IN EVERY AREA OF THE
COUNTRY THAT WE DESIGNATE AS
METROPOLITAN.

"OUR PEOPLE WERE NOT PREPARED FOR THIS
PSYCHOLOGICALLY, NOR WHERE THEY READY
FOR THE TERRIBLE SHORTAGES THIS OIL EM-
BARGO HAS CREATED, WITH PANIC BUYING.

"AS YOU KNOW, MOST OF THE STORES ARE
EMPTY. GAS STATIONS ARE CLOSED FOR EX-
TENDED PERIODS OF TIME. WE HAVE
DECLARED, THROUGH THE PRESIDENT, A WEEK
OF VOLUNTARY VACATION FOR EVERY CITIZEN.
THE PRESIDENT HAS TOLD CONGRESS THAT TAX
CUTS WILL BE LEGISLATED FOR EVERY WEEK OF
LOST WORK FOR THE PEOPLE IN THIS CRISIS.
'WHATEVER YOUR SALARY IS FOR THE WEEK,

YOU CAN DEDUCT THIS FROM YOUR TAX RETURN NEXT SEASON. THAT IS NOT MUCH HELP NOW, BUT IT WILL BE LATER, SAID GOVERNMENT SPOKESMEN.

"PLEASE STAY HOME AND SHARE WHAT YOU HAVE WITH YOUR FRIENDS AND RELATIVES. RELIEF IS ON THE WAY. THIS STATION WILL AN-NOUNCE WHEN AND WHERE, AND HOW RELIEF IS COMING—AS SOON AS FOOD AND FUEL ALLOCATIONS ARE PROVIDED BY OUR GOVERN-MENT.

"WE REPEAT, STAY AT HOME. RELIEF IS COM-ING FOR THOSE SUFFERING THE MOST. CALL YOUR LOCAL NUMBERS SHOWN ON THE SCREEN NOW, IN THE VARIOUS AREAS OF THE COUNTRY, IF YOU ARE IN DIRE NEED OR HAVE AN EMERGENCY NEED FOR MEDICATION, FOOD, OR POLICE. PLEASE STAY ON THE LINE—THE COM-PUTER WILL PUT YOU THROUGH. MOST LINES ARE JAMMED. SPECIAL EMERGENCY SQUADS ARE SET UP TO AID THE DISTRESSED AND ELDERLY FIRST."

Your Reaction

You are stunned! You sit back, take your wife's hand, and look at her shocked and amazed at what is going on. You thank God that you read books on what was coming, and you say to your wife,

"Darling, I'm so glad we did our homework. We're here, safe with the children, and when I think of what we have here, I have to thank God and our instincts that we bought the food and the gold coins."

"Where are the guns, dear?" Your wife asks anxiously.

"Right in the kitchen, loaded and ready, when I need them."

"Do you think we're really safe?"

"Definitely. I've checked and rechecked everything. All

is safe and secure, and we are hidden exceptionally well from anything dangerous." You pause, reassuring your wife.

"Trust me, darling . . . we planned for this."

You sit back and reminisce momentarily. You and your wife are safe with your children, who love what is going on outside, not aware of the dangers that have developed in America's economy or way of life.

You remember with a flush of happiness that trip to Hawaii and the books you meanderingly picked up to read while lying in the hot Honolulu sunshine.

You read a book on the coming economic disorders—all about why you should own gold and silver coins as the dollar was dying along with other world currencies.

You read other books along the same line that week and determined to follow the stock market and the gold reports.

To your consternation, as you watched the gold prices day by day, even while on vacation, and then back in the office reading the *Wall Street Journal* (a paper you had rarely bought before), gold prices were soaring (with an occasional dip), and silver was reaching for the stars, while the dollar was steadily declining. You watched the M1 and M2 reports and saw too much money being printed weekly by the FED.

You watched for weeks as it slowly built in your mind. You wished you had bought the precious metals while on vacation. Now it was two months later. Gold has leaped over 23 dollars per ounce on the open market. You had over 10,000 dollars in the bank, drawing less than 8 percent this year in interest, but inflation was at least 12 to 16 percent already? You knew you were losing money by leaving your dollars in the bank.

Suddenly you moved. You went to the bank and withdrew your money while listening to them tell you, "Substantial penalties will be inflicted on the interest, because you are withdrawing it between interest-setting periods."

You smile now, remembering what you said to the lady:

"Ma'am, perhaps you don't know it, but I am losing at least 8 percent this year in inflation alone, to say nothing of what I'm losing by not having this money in gold NOW."

You took the money and went to a local precious-metals dealer that you had already checked out. He had been in business a long time.

You bought 10,000 dollars worth of South African Krugerrands, beautifully packaged. You put them in your briefcase and walked back to the office.

From that exciting day on, you watched the markets, read the papers, and saw exactly what was happening to gold, silver and real estate in your community.

Real estate continued to boom for a while. Then came the slump. No one could afford the interest rates for mortgages. Homes were "out of sight" in pricing.

You could buy the same type of home in British Columbia or Oregon that you could get in California, for 40,000 dollars less!

Then your areas started to slip too. Real estate values had to correct in order for people to buy.

You finally put your home up for sale, after much conversation between you and your wife, and sold it for 37,000 dollars more than you paid four years earlier.

You now had 62,000 dollars in cash after the first mortgage was paid off.

You convinced your wife that living in a leased condominium for a while, with its pool and recreation room, plus schools nearby for the children, wouldn't be too bad a change.

Demand for silver has been unusually high, especially as you discovered that supply was lower than demand for the first time in years.

You now bought more gold, 10,000 dollars more. Some of the cash you used for food, provisions, a snowmobile, and all the things you would need for your "home away from home."

Your retreat has three rooms for sleeping, and is enhanced by a large open kitchen-dining area and living room with a large open fireplace.

It is not big, but it is adequate, warm, and cozy. You are leasing it inexpensively from an old-timer who will not be using it again. He thinks you are going to buy it soon.

Your gold has nearly doubled, and your silver has more than tripled in value.

You are listening via radio to the value of gold and silver on the commodities market right now. You just made much money today!

All of this is because you were smart enough to plan ahead. Even the food you bought has doubled in price since the shortages set in three weeks ago!

Prices for food, gold, silver, and many other products are going crazy. Everybody wants them.

The government is issuing more printed money by the day to keep up with inflation. That's a laugh. You know that this is the very reason we have inflation in the first place. Now they are creating more inflation.

Prices are skyrocketing all over the nation. No one knows where it is going to stop. Everyone is predicting a massive depression in order to counteract the inflationary spiral.

YOU ARE READY FOR EITHER HYPERINFLATION OR DEPRESSION.

Gold, silver, food, and a roof over your head are the things you need to survive this calamity and to come out on top financially.

Should you and your family physically survive, *and you will,* for you are prepared, YOU WILL BE ABLE TO BUY THE WHOLE STREET WHERE YOU LIVED, IF YOU CARE TO, WITH THE TERRIBLY DEPRESSED PRICES SOON TO COME, AND WITH THE INCREASED VALUE OF GOLD AND SILVER, AS CON-

SUMERS ONCE AGAIN DO WHAT HISTORY HAS OFTEN PROVED—TURN TO HARD MONEY IN THE TIME OF CRISIS!

Fifteen Important Facts About Gold

1. Gold and silver have never failed in times of recession, depression, and government collapses. They have never failed in 6000 years of time!

2. Gold nearly doubled in price in one year.

3. Over the long haul of years, even when real estate was performing well and blue-chip stocks were running fairly high, gold outdid them all in terms of long-term, permanent values.

4. Gold has been the greatest store of value since the beginning of commerce, way back in the days of Moses and Abraham, and before them.

5. Gold has a strange mystique about it that no other precious metal has, with silver running a close second in appreciation as hard money.

6. Gold made the aware people rich as governemnts rose and fell.

7. Gold enabled thousands who possessed it to come out of depressions owning far more than they did before the crash came.

8. When the dollar goes down, gold goes up.

9. As governments go deeper and deeper into national debt, and their balance of payments grows worse; gold goes up in value weekly.

10. Because of gold's short supply with so many governments and people wanting it, its price has to go up as demand grows and the supply diminishes.

11. Gold is also universally accepted as the best store of value.

13. Gold is the foremost metal of the arts—the one metal more desired by all mankind, as exemplified in man's quest for gold in every age.

14. Gold will not be replaced by any other metal known

to man in this age of science for the plating of delicate electrical circuits and components and as an anticorrosion measure now commonly performed in electronics, computers, and aerospace technologies. Dental, jewelry, and artistic uses and demands are up tremendously as the world population and affluence grows in certain areas.

15. More people want gold now than ever before in human history, but THERE IS JUST SO MUCH TO GO AROUND. *Get some* NOW.

The Value of Silver

Our friend in his cabin, saved from city problems, had not only bought gold, but also three bags of silver, and had made a bundle by doing so. Silver more than tripled his investment money by the time he hit the woods for safety.

Let me tell you why to buy and hold onto your gold and silver, and what the basic difference is for investment and survival purposes as we get closer to the coming oil war.

You buy gold for larger investments, for a larger amount of money, and you hold it in as small a physical space as possible. Gold is easier to store than silver. It is not in large, bulky bags. It is not as heavy as a bag of silver, if you compare the same amount of money in gold as in silver.

Gold is for larger amounts of money invested. Gold is for larger purchases that you will want to make during the crash and during the war.

Things like a car, house, RV, boat, machinery for business—anything that takes large amounts of money (by comparison with groceries, for instance)—you would use your gold for.

It is especially great for saving large amounts of cash in a small space. One hundred thousand dollars in silver would take a much larger space than the same amount invested in Krugerrands, for instance.

Silver is for smaller amounts of money, to be used for smaller purchases during the crisis period.

You would not take a bag of silver to buy a car or a house (although you could, and some people might).

Silver is for milk, bread, meat, clothes, medicine, gas, oil—smaller purchases.

Let's assume the dollar dies as predicted. The crash is on; the dollar is buying very little. The oil embargo has hit with all its fury. Monetary confusion is everywhere. There is talk about the government producing new money soon. People cannot get their money out of the banks because they are closed for a "short period" as required by the government.

Millions of people did not get their money in the 1929-33 crash. The banks went bankrupt, or closed for months, and so did safety deposit boxes!

You would not buy gas or oil or any smaller purchase with gold coins. You would be seen with the gold and perhaps robbed. No storekeeper could give you adequate change. You wouldn't want his change anyway, since it would be in the currency of the nation at the time.

Instead, you would use silver coins—quarters, dimes, and maybe a 50-cent piece or so. You might take several of them, depending on the price of food and the value of silver.

But rest assured that the silver content of that money will please the storekeeper and owner. Owners of businesses right now are accepting gold and silver coins at their current value!

You will not have any trouble exchanging your silver quarters for groceries. Businessmen will recognize that what you are presenting them with will outlast the dollar in value, and is going up in value!

SILVER IS GREAT FOR AN INVESTMENT RIGHT NOW. It is actually making more money than gold currently.

The reason for this is that there is now a greater DEMAND for silver than SUPPLY. Nations, multinationals, big business, and individuals are into silver more than ever!

Ten Reasons to Buy Silver

Here are 10 reasons why our foregoing family man bought three bags of silver.

1. At the present rate of silver production and consumption, the above-ground supplies will run out in ONE YEAR!

2. Silver is in short supply now, and the supply is getting smaller as industrial, military, and monetary uses increase monthly!

3. Silver is inflation insurance, depression insurance, and old-age insurance. It is better than any retirement plan, especially the government's social security. Had you invested the same amount of money in silver years ago, look where you would be retiring now—ANYWHERE with much money!

4. Silver value is not determined by governments, as is the case of paper monies. Silver stands alone as the second most precious metal known to man. It carries its own value regardless of governments, legislation, and wars.

5. Silver is the second most workable metal known to man, and is used in hundreds of ways and industries, without any metal to take its place even after 6000 years of usage.

6. Silver has an innate whiteness and reflectivity about it, and as a result entire industries are built around it. In no way could tin, for instance ever take its place.

7. Demand for silver will more than triple as industries and governments anticipate harnessing solar energy for mankind as a substitute for oil. Silver is the one metal they must use to do this.

8. Every computer, radio, TV, jet, airline, submarine, rocket, and spaceship, as well as the entire photography industry, use silver in their electrical and electronic systems.

9. It is honestly estimated that in the decade of the eighties the manufacture of TVs and cassette recorder-players could use more than twice the silver than is now

being produced annually!

10. For over 100 years silver has been in an oversupply position, but now, due to everexpanding uses of silver, the oversupply is gone. It has been over 45 years since a major discovery of silver has been found. This means huge profits to those holding it, as supplies dwindle and demand soars!

What to Store for the Coming War

As you sit down and determine what your family needs monthly in meats, vegetables, fruits, and salads, you can come up with what you would need for a two-year period.

In the event of the oil war directly affecting the United States, you have to consider the possibility of enemy missiles landing near where you are going to live. If they land really near there will be nothing for you to consider! But you can help avoid this by considering what is being said in this book.

If the worst does not get you or yours, thank God for it. But you must look out for nuclear fallout. Dust particles filled with death-dealing atoms are capable of killing you instantly. Or if filtered out, they could kill you and yours over a period of time as you absorb them into your system.

You will hear the radio broadcasts as to where enemy missiles have fallen. You will know if the winds will blow ill for you. If you are inside and well-protected, it may take a great deal of time for the fallout to blow over you. You have to eat and live on.

Consider this when you are accumulating food and necessary products for sustenance at your retreat or wherever you are going to live.

I believe that you should secure two year's supply of food for each member of the family. Perhaps you cannot afford to do all this at one time. There are ways that you can secure foods on a weekly and/or monthly basis and be storing it consistently now. You can pay for it as you go, rather than in one lump sum.

DO SOMETHING NOW. THE LONGER YOU WAIT, THE MORE EXPENSIVE THE FOOD WILL BE, AND THE HARDER TO FIND. SACRIFICE SOMETHING ELSE RIGHT NOW, AND BUY YOUR HEALTH AND SAFETY FOR THE NEAR FUTURE. I AM TALKING TO YOU ABOUT YOUR HUMAN SURVIVAL—YOUR FAMILY'S SURVIVAL!

Please remember that if worse comes to worst, you will not be able to fill prescriptions. So get some extra prescriptions filled now.

THINK of the things you will want that might not be in supply at all. BUY them now.

If you plan for the worst, and it does not come, you are prepared but will not have to use everything. That is good. You can share what you have with many others. If you plan for the worst and it does come, you are ready for anything. It is better to have too much than too little, when you cannot get any more!

The worst thing that could happen is that you will have food and provisions left over to eat and enjoy later! But I doubt that this will ever be the case. There will be many mouths to feed.

Your Greatest Security

BUT YOUR GREATEST SECURITY is not food and the necessary provisions I have outlined. YOUR GREATEST SECURITY IS HAVING GOD ON YOUR SIDE, THROUGH IT ALL. See Proverbs 3:1-5.

Remember, no matter where you are coming from spiritually or religiously, GOD CARES FOR YOU AND YOUR FAMILY. Perhaps you have never given Him much thought, other than at burials, weddings, and Easter, when reluctantly you graced the congregation with your presence.

Think about the fact that GOD DOES EXIST FOR SURE! The very scientific law of CAUSE-AND-EFFECT indicates that for every effect in life and in nature, there is a CAUSE. If you look at anything, it had to be caused—your watch, your clothes, your home, your car, and even you. Go back to the earth, life, the heavens, the universe. It all had to have *A CAUSE GREATER IN INTELLIGENCE THAN THE EFFECT.*

Evolution does not fit the scientific law. Only a Divine Being as the FIRST CAUSE does. He alone is the CAUSE GREATER THAN THE EFFECT—IN INTELLIGENCE, POWER, AND ATTRIBUTES.

When you think about all of this, you cannot help but believe that God exists, and if you go further, you will realize that He is a rewarder for those who seek Him.

May I encourage you to read the New Testament and get the story straight about what happened to Jesus Christ and why He died for you.

This is TRUE SURVIVAL. Not only do we get forgiveness of those sins that we are all guilty of, but we also get the GREATEST FRIEND KNOWN TO MAN— Jesus Christ the Savior, who will guide you through the torments to come and help you to SURVIVE.

I wouldn't live without His daily guidance that I get through the Word of the Living God. It is terrific!

Chapter 9
Answers to Questions

There is nothing as interesting or informative as the question-and-answer periods that I have in seminars across the United States, Canada, Europe, and the Middle East.

People have questions. Your questions and theirs have led me further into research and study. It has been a great experience for me in analyzing human beings and in understanding the other man's point of view.

The following questions have been taken from the thousands that have been asked as the most pertinent to the subject of this book.

The answers come from over 20 years of travel in many countries, having analyzed what they are doing and planning, and from the same number of years studying the Biblical prophecies, along with a close scrutiny of modern economics and politics.

1. I have built up a fairly good cash value in my insurance policy over the years. Should I leave it there for retirement, or cash it in and use it now?

ANSWER

Certainly cash it in and use it now to buy gold coins or silver coins, which will bring you a far greater return than interest in the insurance plan. Further, you may never live to use that money. You can put it to good use NOW. You do not want to get it later in devalued dollars, when you could take it now and pay yourself later in escalating gold and silver values.

2. Speaking of insurance policies, an army pilot asked me what he should do with his insurance now. It is whole life insurance, and he is young and having doubts about it.

ANSWER

I told him to cash it in and buy gold and silver with the money. If he feels better with insurance, he should buy only term insurance, which is pure "death insurance" for his family, should anything happen to him. You can buy reducing term insurance, which reduces over the years, as your other assets rise. Or you can buy level term insurance, which is there as long as you pay for it, for those you leave behind. I only recommend term insurance. You can make much more money in gold and silver than you can in making the insurance companies richer with your money.

3. I have put 25,000 dollars away for retirement, plus I will have my social security. Do you think I should just leave it in the bank drawing compound interest until I need it?

ANSWER

Definitely not. Banked money isn't even earning half of what the government says inflation is. And you can bet that if the government says inflation is 14 percent, then it is closer to 20 and 25 percent annually. You are gaining very little in bank interest, and thus are losing money annually as you let that money sit there. Money placed in gold and silver will keep up with inflation and give you a nice return for your investment on top of that. You will have far more to retire on eventually, if we should all live to see that day.

4. All my money and assets are tied up in the house I live in. It still seems to be going up in value, though not as much as it was. Can I leave the money there until I need it, and still be fairly sure that real estate will not fall?

ANSWER

Do not count on it at all. When the depression of 1929 hit, millions of home-owners lost millions of dollars as real estate plunged in value terribly in the depression. It will again. As people begin to feel the pinch of the oil embargo and finally the big shutoff of oil, with many people out of work and businesses cutting back on production and sales, then the money will not be available for mortgages, and people will not have the borrowing ability to get it.

Houses will glut the market. Many out-of-work people will have to sell in order to avoid high payments. Others will sell to avoid taxes and maintenance. Others will just want out because they will see that the rainy day has arrived. There will be more houses than buyers. Prices will fall greatly. Sell now, no matter how inconvenient it might be to move into a rented house, apartment, condominium, or townhouse. You will be glad you did, for you will have much greater peace of mind as you see your money grow in gold and silver instead of drop as real estate values drop. They are already dropping in many places.

5. Inasmuch as you are recommending gold and silver so much, and have been for five years, do you think there will be a correcting in the price, as other economists are stating, and that I should wait and buy later, after it has corrected?

ANSWER

NOW IS THE TIME TO BUY GOLD AND SILVER if you have waited this long. Do not wait any longer if your are in a position to buy. To wait means that you will lose as much or more than you have already lost by not buying five years ago, when it was so cheap. I do not agree with economists who predict a correcting price for gold and silver soon, down to much lower levels. It is possible that prices will lower slightly. But silver is in a position of demand outstripping supply, and so is gold. U.S. auctions are selling less, and even less gold will be on the market next year. I look for great increases in the prices of both metals soon.

6. What other stocks or investments do you recommend to people?

ANSWER

None, other than possessing food and storing it. You will have to pay much more later. I am not a broker. I am just an analyst-writer-speaker who tries to help.

7. I am heavily into government bonds. What do you recommend I do with them?

ANSWER

Sell them as fast as you can. They will only pay you off eventually with devalued dollars that are going to continue to die in purchasing power, as prices go up and the value of the payoffs goes down. Take the money and take your losses now, and invest in gold and silver, where you can completely depend on what is going to happen because of the steady economic decline in the world.

8. Where can I store my gold and silver coins when I buy them?

ANSWER

In a safety deposit box for the short term, while watching the economy of the banks. Someday soon they will collapse under the pressure of a dollar that doesn't buy anything anymore. When I say soon, I mean the possibility of that happening within five years. Another place to store the coins would be in a home safe that is properly installed (cemented into the floor and hooked to a good burglar alarm system connected to your local police department).

9. Do you believe in owning a gun and using it?

ANSWER

Yes. I would not kill, but I would sure scare the person who is stealing from me or attacking me or my family.

10. Aren't you teaching an antibiblical doctrine when you tell Christians to store food and buy gold and silver for the coming time of trouble? Doesn't the Bible forbid this?

ANSWER

The Bible teaches to trust God, and He will supply. It does not teach that I am to spend every nickel I earn now, as I like, whenever I please, assuming that God is going to kill the fatted calf for me and mine when we are hungry and out of food and money. See Proverbs 24:30-34.

God helps those who cannot help themselves.

God helps those who will help themselves.

God does not help those who could help themselves but won't.

When we are told by Jesus to "Seek first the kingdom of God, and His righteousness, all these other things will be added unto you," He meant that we are to put God first in our lives. Then God will show us how to generate income and how to secure food, clothing, and general sustenance. When Jesus said, "Take no thought about what you are going to eat or drink or put on," He meant, "Do not worry about it. Do the best you can to help yourself. God will help you if you are doing your part." He did not mean for us to sit back and wait for one of God's miracles while we do nothing to help ourselves. That's like saying, "If God wants me to have food He'll send it His way." You will starve soon, with that attitude. Solomon said, "Go to the ant, thou sluggard; consider her ways and be wise." They store up in harvest what they want to eat when the snow and ice cover the ground.

We are in the "harvest period" now. Winter is coming fast. Are you ready for it? Have you made preparations for the snow to hit the fields? Farmers understand this better than city folk, who get their pay every Friday. The farmer stores away in the harvest period what he wants to eat all winter, when there is no production in the field. This is what we are to do now for ourselves, inasmuch as we know that the day of reckoning is coming.

11. Do you believe that the "oil kingdoms of America" will ever be broken up to allow the free flow of energy to this country again?

ANSWER

No. They are so interwoven with one another, and are so enmeshed in the general business of the country, and are so in control of banking too, that to even think of them being broken up and their powers distributed to smaller corporations by the government is unconceivable to me. There isn't one leader talking about it, much less campaigning on that platform. It would be political suicide. If you could find one, he would stand alone. He would fail to break them up and would die politically in the attempt. This would drive him out of politics, and his honest views on other things would be silenced. We have gone too far to turn back now. They have us in their control.

12. Do you believe that things like this control will get worse and lead to greater control over human life in America?

ANSWER

Unfortunately, I do believe this. Our government is getting less beneficial to the common man and more beneficial to big industries, banking cartels, and the oil cartel, which we have now in our country. I am not the only one predicting an eventual dictatorship for America unless we have a miracle.

13. Doesn't Biblical prophecy state that there will come an Antichrist dictator, who will take over the world?

ANSWER

Yes, that is definitely predicted in the amazing prophecies of the Bible. A man will arise first as a man of peace (Daniel 11:21-24), then will take control of 10 nations out of the old Roman Empire arena (Daniel 7:1-24; Revelation 17:12), and then, after controlling these 10 nations and building them to a world power, he will use them to control the Middle East oil and Israel. He will take over Jerusalem (Revelation 11, 13) and will set up a government there controlling world oil and world money, especially in the Western nations that will be under his control (2 Thessalonians 2, Revelation 13, 17). The Bible in its prophecies does not state that he will actually take over the whole world. He will *influence* the whole world, but will have jurisdiction primarily over the Western nations. After all, who wants the other nations in the world, with their economic headaches and starving millions?

14. Is it possible that this dictator could take over America?

ANSWER

Yes, he very well could. If he is tied in with the powerful international bankers and oil barons, he could easily control America after a depression and a breakdown of leadership credibility here. When this nation has its depression, the dollar will die and the economy will fall so cataclysmically that anyone offering a solution to the economic ills of this nation and a new viable money backed by gold will be welcomed by all.

15. Do you believe that this nation is headed for a depression as it had in 1929?

ANSWER

Yes, definitely. We cannot keep on spending as the government is spending over and above the tax revenues and not have a depression. The government is financing the expenditures with "false money." It does not exist. It is created out of a computer. More than 70 percent of the money in the country is created out of nothing and will never exist in the form of currency. It is computer money, commonly called credits. Also, there is a terrible amount of money being printed. This is all so inflationary that the bubble will burst with terrible ferocity, and soon! I definitely look for the corrective depression, and I tell people to buy gold and silver and hold onto it, for the day is coming when that may be all that is credible in this country until stability is established.

16. In several of your books and lectures you have mentioned your belief of the Biblical dictators' "new money mechanisms." What is this?

ANSWER

The amazing prophecies of the Bible indicate that this "man of temporary peace" will set up a new type of purchasing power for the common man and a new type of governmental control over wholesaling and retailing. Knowing that his coming is after the establishment of electronic computerization (which is here) and computerized bookkeeping, I am assuming that the reference in Revelation 13:16-18 will be to a type of computerized control of all citizens. If you follow this regime, you will be "marked" or receive a "credit card" on your right hand, enabling you to buy, sell, and be recognized as a loyal follower of his. Without it, you cannot buy or sell legitimately under this government dictatorship. Prophecies state that you could be killed for not taking this mark. Prophecy also states that if you do take it you could be damned by God (Revelation 13:16-18; 14:9).

17. How will this dictator be supported at first, and who will help him get his power?

ANSWER

I look for the same powers that put men into offices today to put him into office. He will control oil, food, and money—and that sounds like international bankers and oil barons, plus politicans that succumb to these internationalists. That's where the money is to put men into office. He will be "part of the family." I am sure he is alive today and just waiting. He will not have to wait much longer. He is not an American, however. The powers that be will select a European or a man from the Middle East, with the emphasis on the former location, rather than the last.

18. Where are the 10 nations that this dictator will take over?

ANSWER

Nine are currently in the European Common Market: Italy, France, West Germany, Luxembourg, Holland, England, Denmark, Ireland, and Belgium. It looks confirmed that Greece will be nation number 10.

19. Will China fight in the next world war over the Middle East?

ANSWER

In my estimation, no. China will not be industrially or militarily ready until the end of the eighties or into the nineties. She will watch with glee as Russia is destroyed and will rise up as a new world power, tying in many Asiatic nations with her. She is now forming the Asian Common Market in the Far East, fulfilling an amazing prophecy in Revelation 16:12—the kings of the East are getting together.

20. Believing in the prophecies of the Bible as you do, do you see this Middle East war removing the Arab Dome of the Rock Mosque, allowing the Jews to build their third temple as predicted?

ANSWER

I certainly do. I believe that it will take this war to do it. The Israelis are ready to build that temple. They feel it will revive Judaism and bring about a greater unification of Jews from everywhere. They are training young Rabbis now for this task and opportunity to serve the people.

21. When do you believe that the coming oil war will break out?

ANSWER

No one knows for sure. But I believe that it will definitely happen in the decade of the eighties. I hope I am wrong, and that it is in the year 2080! But I know it is coming very soon. It will come over demands for energy. That cannot take too much longer.

22. Could there be collusion on the part of the oil barons, the international bankers, and the Communist powers of the Soviet Union to gain their cooperation?

ANSWER

Yes, there could and is. The same men who control the oil industry here in America sit as directors on all major bank boards, as indicated earlier in this book. These same bankers do business with the Communists, as brought out in this book. There has to be some inner working and understanding, or they would never have loaned the Communists billions of dollars, built their industries, and given them our great American expertise right under the noses of the people of the United States. Dollars dictate policies more than principle, nationality, and patriotism.

No doubt promises have been made to "carve up the world" and give everyone their share when the day of victory comes. That day will come during the war, or when the U.S. and Western empires fall into depression, all because of oil manipulation, money manipulation, and political manipulation being implemented right now.

23. Do you believe this oil war is inevitable?

ANSWER

Yes. There is no force on earth strong enough to stop it. Only an act of God could do this. As governments and men, we are not united enough to stop it. There is terrible confusion among the leaders of America, to say nothing of what is happening in the Middle East.

24. In discussing places to live in the coming storm, you have mentioned Hawaii or the outer islands there as a calm port in which to live during this period. Couldn't a person exist well there with food production, fishing, and no worry about air-conditioning and enemy attacks?

ANSWER

Yes and no! Yes, one could live well there—on an outer island, not too heavily populated. You could grow lots of food, have fruit galore, and fish aplenty. You could probably have an idyllic time of it. But there are potential dangers to this area.

You would not want to live in or near the city of Honolulu, since racial riots and violence are likely to break out. Apart from that, providing you found a spot on one of the neighboring islands that is remote and not densely populated by natives, you could make it. (They make it from the fruit of the soil right now.) You could be affected, however, if the U.S. pulls its fleet out of these waters to fight more effectively in the Mediterranean Sea and Atlantic arena. This could happen, leaving the State of Hawaii vulnerable to enemy attacks—Russia coming down from the North to attack the Pearl Harbor area, with its nuclear storage and armed forces.

If there was ever to be an attack directly against the U.S. and its territories, this would be a prime spot to begin with, as the Japanese thought in World War Two. From that point of view, you would not want to be there.

There is the possibility of large tidal waves, as a result of nuclear explosions and geological upheavals. These islands might be greatly affected then as well. Other Pacific Ocean islands and lands have been greatly devastated by tidal waves and earthquakes.

25. Would Tahiti or the Fiji areas be safe to live in?

ANSWER

Probably as safe as any area apart from tidal waves. If you lived on the higher elevations of the mountains, you would probably be fairly safe there and love it!

26. As a Jew reading all this, I wonder if I should give up my American citizenship and return to the land of my forefathers and fight with them.

ANSWER

Looking at it patriotically, maybe you should. They need you there, that is for sure. But they also may need you here. One of the greatest assets Israel has today is the American Jewish people, who love Israel and the Israeli people. They work hard in America to raise money and general interest and sympathy for the great causes there. You could do either and serve a good cause. It all depends on how you feel in your conscience when you ask the question, Where could I do the most good—raising money and morale here, or being directly involved there on the front line?

27. I am of Arab descent, and I don't like what you are

saying about my people. I understand why they will fight against Isreal. I understand their emotion, their motivations, and their needs. But you say they're going to lose in this coming great war, and they will be wiped out. What hope is there for my people?

ANSWER

There is hope. They will not be "wiped out," as you said. I have never said that. I do say they will be neutralized militarily, never to fight again. The military will be destroyed, as I see it. The civilians will survive and will build a new Arab race, to live in peace with Israel, each in his own city and country. Biblical prophecy never states the end of the Arabs, the true descendants of Abraham through Ishmael. They will live in peace together, according to Isaiah and many portions of the prophecies.

28. A couple of friends of mine and my wife and I have devised a plan to escape the mainland of the United States in a boat should there be the sincere threat of an all-out nuclear attack by the Russians. What do you think of this escape idea?

ANSWER

If we are threatened by an imminent nuclear attack, any idea is good if it gets you out of the range of the enemy missiles. This sounds acceptable, providing you know how to sail a larger-type boat. A power boat is going to require fuel and servicing much more than a large sailing schooner. But sailing is not easy. You must have lessons in order to know what you are doing. We went sailing once in the Pacific on a 35-foot boat, and it took three men to keep her going, constantly working in that wind, with sails, wheel, and ropes. Providing you can do this, you could certainly live for quite a while on board a vessel of this nature safely and probably unmolested, if it is stocked with food and water.

29. As an employee for may years of a large computer company, I have earned and acquired stocks and in-house

savings with the company. What would you recommend that I do with my savings, which are drawing interest now, and my stocks, which are still making me money today? Should I cash in or wait a while longer?

ANSWER

I can only answer what I would do if I were you. I would cash in now, take any losses that result, and invest the money in food, gold coins, silver coins, and a place of safety to live in during the coming oil catastrophe. As business diminishes (and it is now doing so in almost every area of commerce in the country), your stock dividends will become less and less. Get out now and buy things that mean growth and survival.

30. Is the coming oil war absolutely inevitable for the United States?

ANSWER

The coming oil war is inevitable in and for the people of the Middle East. There seems no other way for the people of the Middle East. There seems no other way out because of the intransigencies of the nations involved and the importance of the issues, which seemingly cannot be resolved at the negotiating tables.

But to say it is absolutely inevitable for the U.S.A. may not be totally correct. We would not have to enter this war if we had developed energy self-sufficiency via the nuclear power we started to develop. But the strong antinuclear power groups and leaders in the country have set back this energy source at least five and probably ten years. Therefore we will not be self-sufficient in energy. We will be forced to fight for what we need to exist on. It will not be a war for luxuries, but for the very necessities of life we use every day. We will not be able to get enough oil from Canada and Mexico to fill our needs (along with domestic production). We will continually be dependent on OPEC sources of energy for this country.

31. Khomeini, Iran's new leader of sorts, is having a

running battle with the Soviets lately. Do you think this could escalate and bring a break in Iran and Soviet trade and commercial interests, especially over oil and gas?

ANSWER

No, there will be ripples in the "pond of peace" between the Soviets and Iran, but eventually the Soviets will win and will exert great control and guidance in the oil fields and perhaps even politically in Iran. I do not look for Khomeini to last long. Though the people are Moslems, you cannot run a modern government and oil economy on the Islamic faith and its rules. Either they will pay token homage to the faith and repair the disunity in Iran and thus produce more oil via a new political unity, or they will continue to struggle, produce less oil, and listen to Khomeini, until someday his rule will end in probable assassination by a radical left-wing group.

32. **I am a Jew and believe in the coming of the Messiah. I know that you think your Christ and my Messiah are the same, but whether that is so or not is not of any consequence to me now. Do you see the Messiah coming in our lifetime as a result of the fulfillment of many prophecies?**

ANSWER:

Yes. I believe that Jesus Christ, according to the Old and New Testaments, is the Messiah. I also believe that He will return in our lifetime. To be too specific as to when would be foolish. "No man knows the day nor the hour, but the Father Himself." I believe, for various reasons related to fulfilled prophecies of the Bible, that He will come within the twentieth century—maybe sooner than later. I'm ready for Him, and I certainly hope you are too!

Chapter 10
What To Watch For Next

The two key words for you and me are WATCH and WORK.

WATCH for all the indicators telling you what time it is politically, militarily, and prophetically.

WORK for all the things you will need in order to survive what is coming, and work quietly, efficiently, and with great resolve so that nothing will detour you from this goal of family preservation and preparedness.

While you are weekly acquiring the things you will need and are storing them away safely and secretly, KEEP YOUR EYES OPEN FOR THE FOLLOWING EVENTS, SITUATIONS, AND OPPORTUNITIES, AND ACT ACCORDINGLY.

This is my personal list of events to look for, events that will tell me what time it is in world affairs, thus letting me know when to act, and how.

Keep this list handy, and check the items off as you see them transpiring on the world and local scene. You will find many of them happening as you watch the news on TV.

Other items will pull you out of your seat as you read them on secondary pages of your newspaper. Some items you will find in the news magazines, telling the stories of world news with clarity and detail.

You can also find them out immediately by reading my newsletter that is sent to many people, alerting them to what is going on NOW.

Here is the list for watching and checking.

1. First and foremost to watch for will be disagreements in the Arab-Israeli Peace talks. This will be a signal to you that we are turning into the homeward stretch.

2. Look for very tough negotiations on the part of all who are trying to get Israel to grant full autonomy for the Arabs on the West Bank of the Jordon area. Also look for hotly debated disputes over the return of Jerusalem to the Arab regime.

3. Watch for the Arabs to walk out after a heated dispute concerning Israel's intransigency over Jerusalem. Israel will not give it back.

4. Watch for Israel to stage a walkout if the Arabs presume to bring the PLO representatives to the peace talks. The Israelis call this group the "Palestinian Murder Organization."

5. Eventually the Israeli government will allow the PLO into the talks, with some concessions on the part of the Arabs, such as the PLO not being able to vote on the issues at stake (although they will be able to speak their mind).

6. Watch for limited autonomy to be finally granted to the PLO on the West Bank, but only if some neutral government can police it. The Israelis will not trust the powers of the U.N., citing the situation in Lebanon, thereby proving that the U.N. is incapable of keeping the peace.

7. Not wanting the Israelis to carry the big stick throughout the newly created country, the Arabs will then continue their oil pressure on the United States and others, to force Israel into total compliance with Arab demands. They will talk tough about oil cutbacks. The psychological impact of knowing this could come will jar the U.S. into terrible cutbacks in production. Consumption of many products and a sudden crash buying of food, water, and necessities will panic the population. The stores will not be ready for this kind of buying of emergency items. But you

will already have these things.

8. Watch for this pressure on the United States to develop rather soon, in the eighties. The Arabs will lose no time in utilizing the oil weapon against the U.S. The reason? The longer they wait, the more oil the U.S. could buy and store, and the less pressure the Arab moratorium on oil selling would have. They will act fast. You had better act fast too!

9. Watch for the panic news to hit America below the belt. We are not ready for this potential deathblow to our economy, industries, and way of life. There will hardly be any industry not affected. When you hear and see the panic stirring and starting, you should be high and dry away with your family—gone to the retreat and safe.

10. Let's assume that for one reason or another you could not leave your home, apartment, condo, or townhouse. You did prepare somewhat, however, for the troublesome time coming. You do have some extra food, water, and cooking supplies in case the gas, oil, or electricity goes off. You are at home. You may or may not go to work, depending on your local situation. You see the panic rising. Long lines are at the stores waiting for food right off the trucks. Try to get more food *now.* Secure more water supplies. Even plan on relatives coming to live with you, if you are alone. Or a good friend who thinks like you could join you, with his or her provisions. Two can cook and eat cheaper than one. Someone else living with you can provide some companionship, cheer, and protection, especially if you must stay in the city.

11. Get the best of locks on your apartment doors, windows, and sliding doors. *Get the best* if you are staying in the city, as millions will. Do not sacrifice strength and quality of locks for money. Get the finest of their kind. You will love yourself later for doing so.

12. Even before the threat of the Arab cutoff could come a severe cutback of oil supplies by our own ''seven sisters.'' If they feel the problem is going to develop, they

might cut back oil refinement and gasoline sales in order to conserve for the tragedy ahead. When this happens, and you see it happening, you can surmise that they know what is going to happen because of their inside contacts, negotiations, and on-the-spot understanding of Arab emotions, interests, and plans. You should act accordingly.

13. When you hear or read of the Arabs threatening to pull their large deposits out of U.S. banks, understand that they will do so in order to save face should the U.S. not be able to deliver the goods at the negotiating tables regarding Israel. This could panic the banking establishment, but the public will not be aware of what their withdrawals would do the economy.

14. These threats of withdrawals could trigger a run on certain banks connected with domestic investors who want their money out first, before the banks favor the Arabs. Don't get caught with your money in the bank. You could lose your money if the bank went into receivership or bankruptcy, which some would do if the Arabs pulled this off. Don't forget that millions of well-meaning average American people lost everything in the banks in the 1929-33 crash. The U.S. government was not as deeply in debt as it is now, nor were the banks so overinvested in Third World countries as they are now, nor were the American people so much in debt as now. Also, the U.S. had great reserves of gold and silver then. This will be a worse situation by far.

15. Watch for the news of banks suddenly being bought up by other banks or subsidized by the FED. This should signal you that something is going on in the economic community that the news media are covering up and not reporting to the general public. You would most likely get this type of news in the *Wall Street Journal* initially. It could mean Third World nations have defaulted on their enormous loans from these banks and cannot pay, or won't. It could mean that the Arabs are pulling out their money, but the government and banking industries want to

keep it quiet so as not to cause a run on the banks by panic-stricken Americans.

16. Watch for a precipitous drop in the stock market, larger than anything in years. Members of the stock exchange have ways and means of getting the news first. They hear of legislation passing in Congress before the normal public. They hear of it pending, to say nothing of it passing. If you see or hear of a sudden drop of about 75 to 100 or more points of the Dow Jones Industrial Averages on one day, go to the bank and pull out your money—don't wait! It could very well be that the big investors got the news before the press printed it—news of some impending oil disaster or monetary withdrawal that put big business in a very negative position. I certainly look for this to happen soon. Often the stock market is an indicator of what is going to happen weeks in advance.

17. Watch for the Arabs to threaten "dumping of the dollar" for some other currency in the pricing of a barrel of oil. This other currency woulld probably be the ECU (European Currency Unit). They would do this to spite the U.S. over the Israeli situation. They would also do it as the dollar is dying (the ECU is gold-backed). ECU is the new currency of the European Community, led by West Germany's leader. It is a threat to the dollar because it could take the place of the dollar in Arab oil pricing and other world indexing. It could also take the place of the dollar as the world's ultimate reserve currency someday, as a European fight against the U.S. for not balancing its budget, strengthening the dollar, and cutting exorbitant oil imports. They are talking of it now.

If this calamitous change ever happened to the dollar, the U.S. government would not know what to do. They would have little they could do, and would be plunged into a second-class status overnight, with a complete depression on their hands. The dollar has been the world's reserve currency for some time, and has been the only currency in history to hold this prestigious position. To replace it with the ECU would be disastrous, and you should be in your retreat by the time it happens.

18. Be on the alert for news about a limited war with the USSR. News like this, even the official hint of its possibility, is a leading indicator to you to get the heat on in your secluded cabin. If a limited war were ever engaged in, it would mean that 25 million to 50 million Americans could lose their lives, if not more. Most of these would be affected by the fallout hours and days after the missiles strike their targets. You will have to be on the alert for wind patterns, even if you do not live in an area affected by the missiles themselves. A call to your local bookstore will enable you to secure maps indicating where these bases are. That is where you do not want to live!

Watch for special buys on food. Very often you can save almost half the cost of canned goods by buying a case or two at a time, and by watching for the specials advertised.

20. Watch for specials on freeze-dried foods and dehydrated foods, advertised in many magazines, papers, and special food magazines and publications. You can write for much of this and get in the mail all you would need for several months.

21. Gold is an index to the future. When you see gold rising fast (faster than it is right now), you know that the insiders realize there is panic coming in the monetary systems.

The reason gold is going up so fast is that public confidence in the dollar and the government is going down commensurate with the rising confidence in the yellow metal.

Never has the stock of an administration dropped so much as with this current leadership.

FED deflation of the currency brought on the 1929-33 depression. They knew what they were doing. In 1928 things were good. The economy of the country was in a boom state. The stock market was flying. Millions were living well. Then suddenly the FED pulled the plug and deflated the amount of money that went into national circulation. Overnight this stopped production and produced the depression. Many people knew this was going to happen, and pulled out while prices were high in the marketplace. They made their killing just before it all ended, as planned.

22. Watch for jumping values in the silver market, too. It is hard to believe even now that silver is moving so fast. There are many industrial and military uses for silver, to say nothing of jewelry. No new silver finds have been discovered in 45 years. And there is no substitute for silver for workability and high sheen. Supplies above the ground are dwindling, demand is soaring, prices are rising, and YOU SHOULD HAVE SOME NOW . . . for survival money. I am most bullish on silver until the depression strikes. Then the price may correct a little as demand for industrial usage slackens, but that slack may well be taken up by the demand for silver as money.

23. WATCH FOR THE FED TO PRINT MORE AND MORE USELESS PAPER MONEY. It isn't useless yet, but is losing its usefulness every week as they print more and it is worth less. When the government fights inflation, they cut back in the money supply for the nation and raise interest rates. When they fight recession, they produce inflation by turning the presses on, thereby creating monetary confusion, nationally and internationally. When they turn the presses on and then raise the prime lending rate, they are doing so to help government and its budget, for the people cannot afford to borrow the expensive but available money. The government gets it, and it finally winds up in the banks creating inflation by virtue of its overcreation and then through the banking laws allowing the Fractional Reserve System to create more money than ever . . . which does not exist!

24. Watch for news regarding the Soviet Union moving large amounts of military hardware to the Middle East, to "train" and "observe" what is going on, supposedly

because they are so "interested in world affairs."

25. Watch for news of Cuban and Chinese "advisors" moving into the Middle East and further into Africa.

26. Be on the alert for news indicating that Turkey is leaning more and more to the Soviet side of many issues involving the world and especially the U.S.A. Turkey will swing in with the Soviets in this war attempt, as they are Moslems. All Moslems will stick together in this war. It will come at first as a fiery "holy war against infidels." They want Jerusalem back and they want a revival of the Islamic faith. There is nothing like a war in the name of Allah and of Mohammed in order to take the "Holy Land of Islam" back from Zionist Jews (and their allies) and to unite a divided people of many areas and backgrounds. This war will unite them all, except hopefully the Egyptians, who have vowed to stay out.

But if President Sadat were assassinated, and a left-wing radical opposing Israel ruled the country of Egypt, the lather could be whipped up among many Egyptians to follow their Allah to the war. This would be especially true if the new leaders of Egypt merely said, "We have tried, we have done our best, but to no avail. Israel will not give an inch. We have no choice but to join our brothers and fight the Jews."

27. Watch for indiscriminate proliferation of nuclear power. Pakistan (the latest nation to secure it) could very easily pass it on to other Arab states, such as Libya, where it would be in very dangerous hands, along with Syria and of course the PLO. Pakistan is a Moslem state, falling in line with the Arab world in an anti-Israeli stance. Trouble will brew rapidly in the seething pot of the Middle East when the Syrians and PLO declare along with Libya that they have nuclear power to use militarily.

28. Tragically, we can watch for the United Nations to report a rise in world hunger and famine. Nothing could be more terrible for those involved. This increased world hunger and tragic famine will come in certain areas as a

result of OPEC pricing of oil. Oil is just too expensive for the Third World countries to buy and use.

29. When you read that the U.S. government suspects the Soviets of abusing the SALT II Treaty by building more missiles, tanks, ICBMs, and submarines than the treaty calls for, get ready for the Soviets to act in a belligerent manner. Once this starts it will not end until the war in the Middle East breaks out.

30. The Soviets will get belligerent and hostile toward the United States over our Israeli policies and our lack of progress in pressuring Israel to comply with Arab demands. Watch for this, and know that we are very close to the end of peaceful negotiations and are very close to parties walking out and negotiations ending. War could come soon.

Chapter 11
My Hope

Many people believe we are going to have this calamitous Oil War soon. They are trying to prepare themselves and to prepare others. This is my attempt, and I trust that you will profit by this book and others with whom you will share it.

If thousands read this book and take cover, here or there as suggested, and live to see the new day of peace that is coming, I will be thrilled and much rewarded.

If only one family is helped by this presentation to preserve the lives of that mother and father and precious children, then that too will make me glad for the effort of writing and researching this book. Who can place a value on one life, one family, that can start the world again with peace, love, and equality for all?

I do believe that the world will survive. Some have taught annihilation of all. That will never happen. Millions will live on. Millions will die.

We will see the day that the prophet Isaiah wrote about so clearly when he said,

> *They shall beat their swords into plowshares,*
> *and their spears into pruning hooks;*
> *nation shall not lift up sword against nation,*
> *neither shall they learn war anymore (Isaiah 2:4).*

> *In that day shall there be a highway out of Egypt to Assyria, and the Assyrian shall come into Egypt, and the Egyptian into Assyria, and the Egyptians shall serve with the Assyrians. In that day shall Israel be the third with Egypt and with Assyria, even a blessing in the midst of the land, whom the Lord of Hosts*

*shall bless, saying, blessed be Egypt my people, and
Assyria the work of My hands, and Israel My in-
heritance (Isaiah 19:23-35).*

TRUE SURVIVAL DEPENDS PARTLY ON
PHYSICAL PREPARATIONS AND PARTLY ON
SPIRITUAL PREPARATION.

A very rich lady met me one day in a seminar and said,
"All my life I have had Christianity in my head. I have
thought about Jesus Christ and His life and death and
resurrection. I believed in all of that without hesitation,
but it never did anything much for me. Today, after pray-
ing the sinner's survival prayer with you in this aud-
itorium, is the first time that I realized what salvation really is. I have transferred a historical Christ and religion
from my head to my heart. Now I know I am truly a Christian, believing in and on the Lord Jesus Christ."

Perhaps *you* would like to pray the Survival Prayer with
me now, as I have with thousands after a live presentation.
If these things happen as predicted in this book, we will all
want a prayer to rise up into God's presence for our survival and the survival of our families and loved ones.

My Survival Prayer

DEAR GOD IN HEAVEN,
  I COME TO YOU BELIEVING THAT YOU ARE
THERE, LOVING, CARING, AND SEEING ME NOW.
I BELIEVE IN YOU. I BELIEVE IN JESUS CHRIST,
WHO DIED FOR MY SINS, AND FOR THE WORLD'S.
I BELIEVE IN HIS RESURRECTION FROM THE
DEAD. I CONFESS MY SINS AND INIQUITIES TO
YOU. I AM SORRY FOR MY SINS.
  I ACCEPT YOUR DIVINE FORGIVENESS FOR ALL
MY SINS. I ACCEPT YOUR LOVE; I ACCEPT YOUR
POWER TO HELP ME. I PUT MY FAITH IN GOD. I
PLACE MY TRUST IN JESUS CHRIST AND HIS
SACRIFICE FOR ME.
  I THANK YOU FOR TOUCHING ME NOW. I

THANK YOU FOR REACHING OUT TO ME THIS VERY MOMENT. I THANK YOU, GOD, FOR CARING FOR ME AND CHANGING MY HEART AND MY LIFE FROM THIS MOMENT ON.

I THANK YOU FOR TAKING ME INTO YOUR FAMILY OF MILLIONS OF BELIEVERS.

MAKE ME STRONG TO OVERCOME ALL TEMPTATIONS. KEEP ME FILLED WITH FAITH AND OPTIMISM IN THE MIDST OF EVERY TRIAL AND DISCOURAGEMENT. MAY I GROW STRONGER THROUGH THEM ALL.

I LOOK TO YOU IN FAITH AND TRUST FOR THE SURVIVAL OF THE FUTURE, COME WHAT MAY. ALL I HAVE I PLACE IN YOUR CREATIVE HANDS. SAVE MY FAMILY AND MY LOVED ONES. MAKE ME A TOOL IN YOUR HAND TO REACH THEM AND OTHERS.

I COMMIT ALL I HAVE TO YOU. I KNOW THAT YOU WILL PRESERVE ME TILL IT IS MY TIME TO MEET YOU IN HEAVEN.

I THANK YOU, DEAR LORD, FOR MY SURVIVAL PHYSICALLY, AND MOST OF ALL, FOR MY SURVIVAL SPIRITUALLY.

I PLEDGE TO READ THE BIBLE DAILY AND FEED ON IT IN MY SOUL. I PLEDGE TO PRAY DAILY AND MAKE PRAYER AN UNBURDENING PLACE FOR MY TRIALS AND TESTS, AND A PLACE OF GAINING STRENGTH AS I TALK TO YOU HONESTLY, ON MY KNEES.

I PRAY FOR THE WORLD I LIVE IN, THAT IT WILL KNOW YOU, AND THAT PEACE WILL COME SOON INTERNATIONALLY, AND THAT MILLIONS WILL KNOW CHRIST AS PERSONAL SAVIOR BEFORE THE END COMES.

THY WILL BE DONE ON EARTH, AS IT IS IN HEAVEN. THY KINGDOM COME SOON. IN JESUS NAME, AMEN.

A FINAL WORD . . .

When I first started to write this book, Iran had cut back on oil deliveries, but had not yet taken the hostages and produced the furor in our nation. More oil cutbacks are coming, as just promised by a "getting-united" Arab world. Oil prices have been hiked again by OPEC, which in turn is terribly inflationary for the whole world.

At the time of this writing, gold is well over 700 dollars for a South African Krugerrand coin—the coin I have consistently recommended for years as universal money, as a tremendous way to make money and the best way to save your savings and retain your lifelong earnings and investments.

The world is getting ready for THE COMING OIL EXPLOSION. When this strikes, it will strike suddenly and will penetrate the living style of every North American.

Drastic changes will appear in every industry. Unless you have made private plans and have secured provisions for yourself and loved ones, you will be left holding an empty bag.

Just remember these startling facts:

1. The stock market is not growing appreciably at all.
2. Gold is soaring in price.
3. Silver is leaping to unparalleled prices.
4. Crime is skyrocketing and will continue to do so as many people are laid off from work.
5. Drug addiction is increasing, and so are mental disorders, as many people cannot cope with the changes.
6. Political confusion in Europe and North America is growing (as opposed to political unity and respect).
7. In many areas real estate is slipping in price.
8. Wages are not keeping up with the rate of inflation.
9. The purchasing power of your earned dollars is less now than five or ten years ago. Even though you may have had several raises, YOU ARE EARNING LESS NOW IN TERMS OF WHAT YOU CAN BUY.

THIS ALL MEANS THAT WE NEED TO BE PREPARED FOR:

1. War.
2. Economic breakdowns in America that affect us all.
3. Political confusion if not outright dictatorship.
4. Hard times financially.
5. Shortages in everything we use and need.
6. Terrifying news about terrorists, crime, and famine.
7. Unparalleled oil shortages, creating gas rationing, heating oil shortages, and energy crises throughout our country.

THIS IS WHAT YOU NEED TO DO:

1. Prepare yourself financially for the DEATH OF THE DOLLAR. Buy gold and silver coins and hold them till the hour when you really need them.
2. Buy a one-year store of food (dehydrated or freeze-dried) for each person in the family. This is LIFE INSURANCE at its best.

THINK ABOUT THIS: WE ALL HAVE PLANS ON—

1. Life insurance.
2. Auto insurance.
3. Health insurance.
4. Homeowner's insurance.
5. Our burial.
6. Our estate.
7. Our children's education.
8. Our business ventures.
9. Our retirement.
10. BUT WE DO NOT PLAN TO EAT TOMORROW IF ANY EMERGENCY COMES TO THE FOOD SUPPLY OF THE NATION! TO BUY FOOD TODAY IN ORDER TO EAT TOMORROW IS LIFE INSURANCE FOR YOU AND YOUR FAMILY.

If you would like us to help you get information on where to buy gold or silver or survival food, or if you wish a list of my cassettes on many subjects and books on world events and what to expect, please clip the coupon below and send it to me. I'll be glad to send you what you request.

DOUG: Please send me the following information as checked:

☐ For survival monetary investments.
☐ Securing gold and silver, and where to store it.
☐ Your books for sale.
☐ Cassette list for subjects you have presented worldwide.
☐ Your personal newsletter on survival.
☐ Please put me on your mailing list.

NAME _____

ADDRESS _____

PHONE _____

For survival food information and supplies call Martens Health and Survival Foods. In California dial toll free number 1-800-822-5984 or if no answer call collect 916-583-1511. Outside California dial toll free numbers 1-800-824-7861 or 1-800-227-1343 or if no answer call collect 414-283-2257 or write P.O. Box 5969, Tahoe City, CA 95730.

SEND ALL MAIL TO:
DR. DOUGLAS J. CLARK
P.O. Box 275
Clearwater, Florida 33517

RECOMMENDED READING

THE CONTROL OF OIL, by John M. Blair (Vintage Press, New York).
THE PAPER ARISTOCRACY, by Howard Katz (Books in Focus, New York).
THE WARMONGERS, by Howard Katz (Books in Focus, New York).
TRILATERALS OVER WASHINGTON, by Antony Sutton (The August Corporation, Scottsdale, Arizona).
PUTTING MONEY TO WORK, by Yale L. Meltzer (Prentice Hall, Inc., Eaglewood Cliffs, New Jersey).
THE COMING REAL ESTATE CRASH, by Cardiff and English (Arlington House, New Rochelle, New York).
HOW TO SURVIVE THE MONEY CRASH, by Doug Clark (Harvest House Publishers, Irvine, California).
NONE DARE CALL IT CONSPIRACY, by Gary Allen (76 Press, Seal Beach, California).
TAX TARGET: WASHINGTON, by Gary Allen (76 Press, Seal Beach, California).